WILLIAM ALSOP AND JAN STÖRMER

Architectural Monographs No 33

WILLIAM ALSOP
AND JAN STÖRMER

A·E· ACADEMY EDITIONS · E&S ERNST & SOHN

Architectural Monographs No 33
Editorial Offices
42 Leinster Gardens London W2 3AN

Editorial and Design Team: Andrea Bettella (Senior Designer);
Nanet Mathiasen, Winnie Nielsen (Design); Iona Spens (Editorial)

Cover: Model detail of Kaufhof des Nordens, Hamburg (photograph,
Oliver Heissner); *Page 2:* William Alsop with a piece of architecture on
his sleeve (photograph, Roderick Coyne)
All illustrative material courtesy of Alsop & Störmer

First published in Great Britain in 1993 by
ACADEMY EDITIONS
An imprint of Academy Group Ltd

ACADEMY GROUP LTD
42 Leinster Gardens London W2 3AN
ERNST & SOHN
Hohenzollerndamm 170, 1000 Berlin 31
Members of VCH Publishing Group

ISBN 1 85490 263 6 (HB)
ISBN 1 85490 264 4 (PB)

Distributed to the trade in the United States of America by
ST MARTIN'S PRESS
175 Fifth Avenue, New York, NY 10010

Printed and bound in Singapore

CONTENTS

Bundanon, New South Wales

MICHAEL SPENS

FUNCTION FOLLOWS FORM?

This new collection of work by the office of Alsop & Störmer represents a part of one year's work in 1993. So it is published as a kind of interim statement. After the dramatic arrival of the Hotel du Département at Marseilles (Headquarters for the Regional Government of Bouches-du-Rhone) on site, on schedule in early spring, things would never be the same. As Alsop said, 'it really does look exactly like the final model'; fulfilment of a long gestation, and seventeen different versions, developed and negotiated over more than two years, into virtual reality.

As this new material goes to print, Alsop is standing in New South Wales, Australia. We are looking at a site at Bundanon, where a centre for the visual and performing arts is proposed on ground given to the Australian nation by the painter Arthur Boyd. A lake, a stone-built homestead, on a plateau in the bend of the Shoalhaven river; and all around, the sounds of the bush. The notebook is already out . . .

Back in Europe, what Alsop somewhat uniquely demonstrated in 1993 has profound implications for future architecture. In his keynote essay Bryan Appleyard is right to start with Marseilles, surely correct in asserting that from there on a new aesthetic formulation emerged in Alsop's work, and that this is particularly asserted in the family of three projects described in this book.

At Swansea, the built form is disarticulated into its constituent embryos; this begs the functions which emerge explicitly, with due celebration, yet in a fundamentally adaptive way. And necessarily, for already in the past month the library facility itself has been hived off: the scheme is designed to survive such revisions at the behest of the client. To many of the other projects in the competition this would have demanded massive revision of the whole scheme. Not with Alsop.

In the projects for Hamburg and Nuremberg, a similar adaptiveness is evident, as will be shown here. These buildings, with Swansea, celebrate changeability: it is even celebrated as a reflection of context, both historical and environmental. There is a growing mastery of form, let alone function – the balance seems assured.

At Hamburg, the critical relationship on one side of the main road, with the 'outside', and also with the listed building adjacent on the other side, was allowed to define the formal envelope without constricting its identity. This process is epitomised by the provocative, multi-coloured glass prow which projects across the entry street.

At Nuremberg, while there is a more obvious legacy from Marseilles, the perceived enigma (what actually goes on in one of numerous World Trade Centres?) seems to be enhanced by the opaque facades of the model, with none of the explicit role definitions offered at Marseilles.

Alsop's architecture is the means of energising the programme through a series of explorations, via painting, notebooks, on to protracted yet decisive on-site negotiations to adjust exactitudes of positioning, colouring and texturing. In 1993, the legacy of Marseilles is in full spate . . . better that it be documented as of now.

As Will Alsop says, 'all the work we do is one work'. Nonetheless the development of his architecture over fifteen years has generated identifiable 'groups' of projects. Early in 1993 it became apparent, as the Marseilles Hotel du Département was visibly rising on the edge of Marseilles city, that a quite distinct family of projects was underway in the London studio; and while they each owe individual debts for the evolution of elements in the Marseilles design, they have formed a clear grouping of design affinities – what Alsop defines as a 'family' of projects.

It is clear that the competition-winning National Centre of Literature, the Hamburg Department Store, and the scheme for a World Trade Centre at Nuremberg have all evolved within some twelve months. But if we trace their common aspects, a corroboration emerges first-hand through the relevant paintings. As Alsop says, the art of painting (in the design process) is akin to 'designing a conversation', not a building.

What is therefore really evident in paintings drawn from the preliminary thoughts for each of these projects is a series of similar conversations. These dwell upon the uncertainties as much as the certainties involved in each project brief and its development. There is an ongoing but never cyclical discussion here. A genetic coding can in a sense be identified by tracking back to these conceptions. More specific still, it has been possible to track a vein of thought that developed in the 1990-91 Museum of Scotland competition as generic, in particular upon the first of the 1993 projects, that for Swansea.

The Edinburgh project was also important in practice history, since it rather dramatically marked the impending split in the practice, between Alsop and his former partner John Lyall. In fact so marked was the division that the practice registered two quite different entries. The Lyall-directed Edinburgh office offered a

highly contextual project; while the Alsop team in London produced what *Building Design* referred to as 'advanced building technology, clarity of volume and typology (which) are characteristic of the original 19th-century museum' (January 14, 1991). In other words rather than searching externally for contextual visual affinities bounced off the immediate urban texture, Alsop himself translated the clarity of technical solution, of the existing building, into its late 20th-century technological equivalent – such an overt statement could only be made by the local separation and full structural expression of the necessities of the various parts, based upon a clear understanding of the requirements' real meaning.

The Museum of Scotland was to be read as a narrative, programmed for future generations. In this direct way it would contribute appropriately to the city's own image. There were four key elements in this, identified in the project submission as the Canopy, the Ark, the Chest and the Well, collectively 'The Grand Pavilion'. Under the massive canopy, suspended from a vierendeel roof structure, itself supported on four massive steel columnar structures, the exhibition hall or 'ark' was suspended. Ancillary galleries, perhaps containing high value objects of special interest, formed a steel-framed block of more conventional design – the 'Chest' of Treasures.

In conformity with the brief, the remainder of the exhibits including heavy engineering structures, were placed at ground level or below ground. A superb library, restaurant and viewing gallery overlooking the city, were contained within the roof structure.

The repository provided was intended to offer an elegant and

secure place for the treasures of the past, yet giving the promise of the future and sharing the conversation with the people of Edinburgh: literally as a result of the advantages of the suspended 'ark', the whole space at ground level could be made accessible to pedestrians. Street events as festival performances could be held (and projected onto screens) in the space below this tabernacle. The project was, as subsequent work has proved, likely to be very substantially cheaper to construct than the post-1970s late-Corbusian scheme actually selected by the jury as winners.

The night effect of the project on the skyline and streetscape of Edinburgh was quite dramatic, rendering the formal clarity of the concept self-evident as it glowed with 'a quiet but distinctive identity'.

This 'work' did not however prove to be wasted; valuable research had been carried out into large structural systems of support and compression and how these could fit harmoniously with tensile structures.

So it happened that the invitation to participate in the competition for the National Centre of Literature was one taken already in motion by the revised Alsop practice. The paintings that flared in Norfolk and in London, with or without Bruce McLean, now conveyed the terms of an open conversation already in sway. How does one represent a culture, a literature, all words, in buildings?

At this point Mel Gooding, connected with Swansea and fully rooted in the culture, joined the discussion (of which both Bryan Appleyard and Bruce McLean were already participants). As will be seen, what emerges is surely a project for a centre as Welsh as it is internationalist in approach.

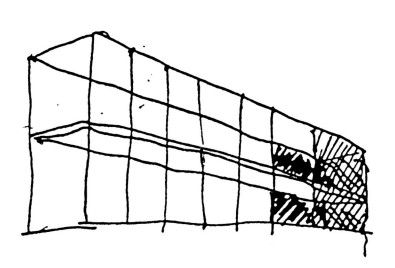

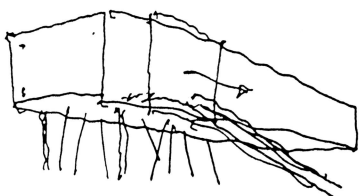

BRYAN APPLEYARD

ARCHITECTURE VERSUS SHOPPING

Will Alsop's 'breakthrough' building – the centre of regional government for the Bouches-du-Rhone region in Marseilles – represented a serious challenge to the small community of global architectural stars. Previously known as a troublesome English maverick, brilliant but sparsely built, Alsop occupied a certain recognisable niche. Clearly he was as good or better than the best, but the small scale of his completed commissions preserved him as an acquired taste, a connoisseur's delight, rather than a real threat to the architectural oligarchy.

Marseilles changed all that. It was a bespoke building combining civic grandeur, political symbolism, public space and office development. It represented a very public, very visible announcement that Alsop the maverick was officially in the major league. This was a competitive threat, but it was also a critical challenge for it meant that the 'official' narrative of 'important' architecture would have to be adjusted to encompass the Alsop story. Yet again a French architectural jury had rocked the boat.

Adjusting the narrative turns out to be a massive rewriting job, for Alsop resists, subverts, even lampoons the critical histories and the fashionable chatter. In maverick exile he has developed an amiably antagonistic posture. He is profoundly un- or rather anti-fashionable and spectacularly incapable of standing still long enough to be regarded as part of a school or movement. Periodically he seems to have been nailed down as post- or neo-modernist, even for one period as a 'lyrical mechanist', however the labels never adhere for more than a week or two and, certainly, they never survive the next project.

This protean progress is, in the contemporary context, perhaps the most subversive element in Alsop's work. The need to label architects – indeed, all artists – is fundamental to the way current criticism operates and architects usually collude with the critics. The most superficial reason for this is commercial. It is calming for a client to feel that he knows what he is going to get if he hires a 'name', disturbing for him if all he is offered is unpredictability. At a slightly deeper level there is the whole culture of fashion that conceives of architecture as a battle of styles: high-tech, post-modern, neo-classical, whatever. Such an approach considers the thinnest film of the building's skin as it would the length of a woman's skirt and then critically positions the architect on the basis of the most elementary style cues. Finally, behind all this there is the rigid historicism of modernist criticism that buildings must be like this: that is what history demands of them. Under this banner the fabulous fecundity of Le Corbusier's buildings is quietly smoothed to a modernist unity so that the artist can be claimed to represent his age, to be true to the false, simplistic historical narrative which even his greatest admirers need if they are to feel safe.

All of this puts enormous pressure on the artist to be one thing, to have certain quickly recognisable attributes instantly evoked by the employment of his name. Inevitably most artists oblige, including, it has to be said, some of the best. They are cornered into conceiving of the superficialities of a style – even the compulsive eclecticism of Post-Modernism – as an absolute. In defence, they begin to elevate the details of that style to something grand, most commonly claiming that it is a 'language'. This, says the high-technician or the neo-classicist, is how we speak.

Such a posture implies a definition of the word 'architect' – he becomes a practitioner, a stylist – and it offers the client the role of shopper: he selects a package of name and style, validated, or perhaps not, by a specific critical rationale. But, if such a cosy, inert relationship does not exist, more is demanded of both sides of the deal. If either deprived of or declining a consistent style, the architect is obliged to explain what he – uniquely – does in more complex terms; equally, the client will have to take on trust the talent he has hired. The immense gain is that the building is freed to be more finely tuned to its function, symbolic and actual, to its site and its real place in architectural history.

The ideal starting point to exploit such freedom is to begin with a certain vacuum, an absence of preconceptions and obligations, an absence as Alsop would put it, of ideas: 'the real crux of it is to be happy with not having an idea at all. That would actually mean that the work has taken over. You don't rely on those things which are highly unreliable called ideas to motivate the work'.

This is a serious heresy because ideas are usually the easiest things to pin down with critical formulae. So, for the critic, that other party to the architectural deal, this featureless, pristine landscape, free of ideas but awaiting inspiration, does not present a soothing prospect. What is he to say of Alsop the architect if Alsop will say so little about himself and persists in being so stylistically, well, moody. What statements can he make if the architect so studiously avoids statement and remains so ruthlessly committed only to an ideal of self-questioning that guarantees sudden changes and capricious directional lurches every few years? The only solution is that each building must be confronted as an object unattached to any predetermined narrative. It will not fit, it insists on expressing only itself. This is a form of art degree zero of the type evoked by Samuel Beckett when discussing the painter Bram van Velde. 'For what,' asked Beckett, 'is this coloured plane that was not there before? I don't know what it is, having never seen anything like it before. It seems to have nothing to do with art, in any case, if my memories of art are correct.'

Robbed of his lifeboat of familiarity, the critic is thrown back on that most frightening of questions: do I like it?

Even springing from an *oeuvre* that does not fit, the buildings in this book are startling for their refusal to fit. For those who in their minds labelled Alsop as, perhaps, 'bizarre' or 'complex', they will come as a shock. These buildings are predominantly rectilinear, they are cool, laid-back, almost, and – a word never previously applied to Alsop – tasteful. They are understated to the point that an idle glance may fool you into thinking they are rather like other buildings. Is, the idle glancer might wonder, Alsop settling down?

The first clues to what is going on here can most clearly be seen in Marseilles. Much of that building is consistent with the image of Weird Will. The baguette-shaped *deliberatif*, the curious palette-shaped decks and the spreading modularity of the plan all carry a signature that is, if not familiar, at least reassuringly strange. But this building has a 'fast' side and a 'slow' side. The *deliberatif* is on the fast side and is to be seen largely by people passing in cars, its impact is calculatingly direct.

In contrast the quality of the building's slow side can be more oblique, less aggressively theatrical. The solution is the cool glass facade riding on top of the huge concrete X-legs. The impact, apart from the quality of the colouring and Brian Clarke's fine art work on the glass, is dependent entirely on proportion. The X-legs are 12 metres high, an obviously exaggerated size for a ground floor in a building of such height, but a size that balances the glass above with an almost classical correctness. 'Simple forms,' Alsop says, 'if you get the proportions right have enormous presence.'

The success of this effect inaugurated the current phase in Alsop's work. Proportion as the sole or dominant architectural tool is a classical ideal and it is clear that the architect is experimenting here with the possibilities of a form of classical impulse. Proportion, used in this way, is a calm, recessive device. It invites rather than demands your attention. It evokes cool, self-possession, confidence.

At Nuremberg, Swansea and Hamburg the impulse has blossomed into cool, self-possessed buildings, all of them intended to be at home and well-mannered in their surroundings. This may seem a long way from Alsop the outrageous maverick who used to scoff at the kind of contextualism that made good architects pay homage to bad buildings just because they happened to be next door. But there is a connection. Immediately before his Marseilles phase, Alsop was playing with a reversal of an old modernist motto. Why, he was asking, shouldn't function follow form? Why should the building as sculpture not be free of the building as practical project? The implication was that the modernist drive to build from the inside out. Producing exteriors celebrating functionality may be the worst stylistic straitjacket of all. It is usually also, frankly, rank hypocrisy: no building can have such a precisely tuned function that its exterior *must* possess one specific appearance. All the real decisions were always aesthetic.

By considering specifically this issue Alsop has identified the central problem of 20th-century style. Deprived of the social, political and religious structures that determined style in the past, the modernists enlisted function as the only rational determinant. The idea of function provided a new rigour, a kind of stripped down wholesomeness that even in its most extravagant high-tech incarnations could always fall back on a functional rhetoric in justification. Of course, this was not the only modernist orthodoxy, but it was the one from which all the others were self-conscious departures and the challenge to which all architects had to respond.

With the pirouettes of attempted escape from Modernism in recent years, the nature of this challenge has become, ironically, more not less acute. The hard modernist question 'why?' still undermines the pediments, porticoes and barrel vaults that have leapt up in our cities. The jokey, unsupported masses of our neo-classicism draw attention to the intellectual and imaginative capitulations that were implicated in their conception.

But Alsop is a kind of aesthete – an unusually robust kind, admittedly – in that he regards art as autonomous. This is not an explicit belief so much as an unspoken assumption in all that he says and does. Such an assumption gives a quite different per-spective on all the crises of style. Form and function, for example, is not a simple equation that magically equals art; rather art is the dominant factor on the left, not the right, of the equation. Equally the puritanical modernist fear of decoration is a relatively trivial matter when set against the demands of art for whatever is right. The 80s battle of the styles becomes, of course, simply absurd, since to adopt of any of those postures would wilfully restrict art's freedom of manoeuvre.

With the demands of autonomous art in the foreground, it becomes perfectly obvious that each building is to be dealt with on its merits rather than on the basis of stylistic or critical injunctions. Equally it became likely that the pursuit of this metaphysical ideal should range through a variety of possible approaches. With the buildings in this book the approach has come close to an ideal of *beaux arts* classicism – architecture as the creation of beautiful objects disciplined by proportion. This ideal of beauty is being tested for its ability to sustain Alsop's private requirement for art.

This points to a profound irrationalism at the heart of Alsop's work and it explains his instinctive unease with the various critical languages that have been used to entrap architecture. All of them threaten to restrict the artist's freedom to change and to experi-ment, and therefore to distract him from his sole obligation – the pursuit of whatever might constitute art in our day, the pursuit of what Wallace Stevens called 'the supreme fiction'.

14

Previous Page: Developmental painting for Hotel du Département, Marseilles; *Above*: Developmental painting for Museum of Scotland, Edinburgh

WILLIAM ALSOP

TOWARDS AN ARCHITECTURE OF PRACTICAL DELIGHT

THE DRESDEN PRINCIPLES
– Building both in the process of design and later under construction should be a celebration.
– The experience of the edifice should lift the human spirit.
– The architect should use any means possible to achieve the above.

Within the confines of these objectives, it is not possible, or desirable to become a slave to a philosophy, style or specific procedure. Instead it is more important to consider yourself as the consumer of the products of architects (and others) before subjecting the world to products born of architectural debate by architects.

RELY ON YOUR OWN EXPERIENCE. LOOK TO YOURSELF
Anything is possible to build, or not build, we could therefore ask the question as to why styles and fashion and methods tend to become common practice within our environment.

The objective is to reach the point where one is liberated from having to answer with a justification, reason or theory. It is enough to say, honestly, 'I don't know' and know this is correct.

Of all the arts, architecture is one in which the artist is expected to be able to talk, reason and justify almost every move. This is because architecture is the art of prediction. The discussions take place around approximations and speculations of a future that does not yet exist. In painting, sculpture and even science there is a tangible result which can be appreciated for itself and therefore open to discussion. Whatever is said, the deed has been done. Architects have nothing concrete, only a strategy and themselves.

WHAT IS THE NATURE OF A DISCUSSION AND WHO IS IT BETWEEN? Everyone has expectations. Society established codes of acceptable behaviour as a method of operating. Everything we do is an agreement, as we should never delude ourselves by thinking that we have ever acted in a completely independent manner (why should we want to?). The nature of introducing anything into the world is collaborative, therefore the nature of what we do is in its essence a compromise. If we are aware of this, we can turn the idea of compromise into a positive energy, as opposed to the common idea that all compromise is a watering down of concept. What happens if compromise is the concept? The discussion is between society and the architect and between individuals in society and the architect.

The question is then how to discuss. Each party contributing to the discussion has expectations and preconceptions. We therefore have to find ways of undermining these as much as possible. This applies to your own as well as others.

I often start by painting. The paint has a life of its own, beyond your control. It is possible to see what you cannot think. The paintings do not have the authority of traditional sealed drawings and as such can be used in discussions. This act is an invitation to misinterpret, extend and corrupt. I often describe this process as designing a conversation, not a building. People must feel relaxed and uninhibited. It is very important that all ideas, objectives and idle thoughts can be voiced and therefore considered. The conversation is open. This same principle is used with the whole team of people involved with changing the surface of the earth and/or strategies of varying known behaviours. Because change is inevitable, and is always a major consideration in any proposition, it is natural that the idea of uncertainty should be built into the design process. My work is never sure of any agreement at any stage of development. It is always important to reconsider projects in part or totality right through the design and construction. This attitude accepts that the task of predicting the future is impossible and as such we can only attempt to make it as real as possible at all stages. A flash of perception ought to be acted on. It is never too late.

All functions can be labelled. When they are labelled they become institutionalised. Architects spend their time worrying about the programme – usually expressed in the form of functions. I prefer the truth about behaviour as this is less specific. 'Eating' can mean anything from grazing, to picnics, to formal restaurants. If the word 'canteen' appears in your brief, it already assumes a particular type of place, which prevents thought and speculation.

LEAVE IT LOOSE UNTIL IT FEELS RIGHT
Every project should be a surprise to both the client and yourself. This implies that one starts afresh with each new work. This is totally wrong. It is vital to build on the experience that you accumulate. There is no need to make the same mistake twice. The point is that all the work that we do is one work and that the development of that work is only possible through an open and direct involvement with society. The challenging of habitual behaviour resulting in an agreement between you and the world is a way forward.

ARCHITECTURE: ONE WAY OF EXPLORING THE WORLD THROUGH WORK – IT MUST HOWEVER ALWAYS BE AN EXPLORATION, NOT A CONFIRMATION.

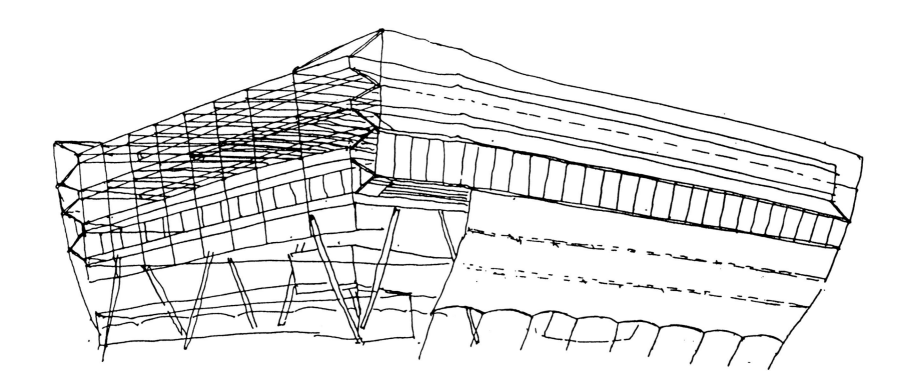

MICHAEL SPENS

THE NATIONAL CENTRE OF LITERATURE SWANSEA

Will Alsop, in winning the competition last February to design the National Centre of Literature, has consolidated a reputation that has been built uncompromisingly upon a clear vision of the next century and the architecture that a more open and diversified society will come to demand more and more frequently. The competition itself may prove to have been a watershed in the succession of a new, different generation of architects, even. Alsop is different in age from the high-tech knights by barely half a generation – but the world which he and a supporting cast of architects, engineers, and artists inhabit is several decades apart from *The Eagle* comic inspired adulation of technical parts that launched 'high-tech' as an architectural connotation.

It is significant that the also-rans in this competition final were, among others, Michael Graves and Stirling & Wilford. But then the project in hand required an understanding of cultural forces, local aspirations, and no preconceptions as to the nature of a seaside provincial city in South Wales. Alsop already had an inkling, since his Cardiff Bay Visitors' Centre attracted some 200,000 visitors in its first year – the ability to attract such a community to the extent that it identifies with the building on offer and even wants to hang onto it. Alsop buildings do not descend on the community from on high. Instead they establish an affinity, a feeling of collaboration in the question of the future.

The competition brief was a remarkably enlightened one, devoid of the usual bureaucratic priorities. The project was to incorporate a major new central library building, but only in its second phase. The initial phase demanded a more challenging array of facilities, including exhibition galleries to accommodate a Museum of the Word, a range of changing displays, an international writers' centre carrying overnight accommodation (libraries are conducive to sleep and dreams), plus a network of activity space, linked also to a cafe/restaurant and a major bookshop.

Here was an extraordinary example, in Britain, of a city council determined to stimulate a wide spectrum of literary culture, yet in a deep relationship not dependent upon adjacent academia. The word in Swansea has been most prevalent when it has sprung from the streets and pubs and bedsits, conscious always of Dylan Thomas (and Richard Burton) in this way, the life of Kingsley Amis as lived hereby is no less relevant, endorsing along the way the predictions of Richard Hoggart (written, it must be remembered, at much the same time as *The Eagle* comic was created). Alsop didn't have that deep knowledge of the place, but he had the intelligence (and humility) to involve Mel Gooding, who comes from deep within.

The result has been a remarkable affirmation of hope in the cultures of tomorrow. Woven into the concept is a full consideration of available cultural networks upon which the physical structure required can enrich and regenerate itself. Fundamental has been the awareness of the city authorities that they have, for a long time, been sitting on seams not just of black gold, but of literary gold. The question was how to extract the resource in a viable way.

At this juncture it is worth recalling that Alsop had, two years past, given due consideration to the Museum of Scotland requirements for an extension. The purpose of the extension, the subject of another competition (but an open one), was the exposition in an accessible manner of the scientific, archaeological, and ethnographic treasures of Scotland in a manner plausible and stimulating to the visitor.

The Alsop scheme, although unplaced in the selection, was a direct precursor of the Swansea scheme. The Scottish treasures were celebrated, enhanced, and made accessible by means of a suspended 'ark' which offered a clear street-level gathering-place at which passers-by could experience, and be drawn into, the vaults of the building – valuable relics were housed in a separated and adjacent 'chest' of more conventional construction. The street-level space could even be curtained-in for temporary exhibition or festival performances. Although the ark had something of the connotation of a tabernacle, the word as such stopped short of *tabulae rasae*. Swansea has posed a related set of problems to those solved by the Alsop Edinburgh scheme.

As Mel Gooding explains, the key factor about the word, so to say, is its very invisibility. This very invisibility of the word had somehow to be borne out, embraced and celebrated. This process at first involves the display of actual books, accessible microfiches of old and wonderful books, and comprehensive electronic archiving of innumerable books. Provision is made for electronic browsing as it is for real browsing. A Red Box, a Tower of Words, and a Tower of Books seemed to be called for.

Since the word has its roots in the streets, as the spoken word (as that once was rooted in the glades and groves of an aboriginal Wales), the basic street geography of the immediate city was a prime consideration in generating the building idea. As at Edinburgh, the clearing of the street level space below the ultimate building was vital in allowing key pedestrian routes to intersect and congregate on the site. A pedestrianisation of local streets was already in sway, but terminating meaninglessly at the edge of the site of the Centre. Alsop was determined to create a 'place' or square under the main accommodation of the building, which would in Phase II incorporate the city library. So the 'songlines' of the city memory could be sustained, and developed this way.

The public library is incorporated, as Phase II, in the two floors above the museum. In the interim following construction of Phase I, the 'roof' would be covered with a temporary fabric weather shield. The libraries would be light and spacious, allowing for both air-conditioning and natural (opened windows) ventilation.

Library design, as such, has always imposed special demands upon architects. Whether in the hands of Plecnik at Ljubljana, or Aalto at Viipuri, one of the key tools employed has to be light, and its subtle and dramatic manipulation. This can achieve special significance on entering the building (as in both the historical examples, and with this building especially). Alsop thus draws the library user into a special relationship with the building, unwittingly he or she is propelled upwards. At night too, when the Centre may be busiest, Alsop has cast a magnetic array of lighting across the interior of the building and its elements, hoping to emphasise its key role in the city, as a beacon for the future. And from the roof (as with the Edinburgh project) users can look out over the lights of the city outside.

Alsop has quite possibly advanced the whole concept of a Centre of the Word into a typological revision which will redefine the identity of the genre. If Swansea can be read as a prototype, then in such circumstances the word and its civilisation connotation becomes, in whatever part of the country or the world, of paramount impor-

tance. Alsop's realisable complex of uses might be infinitely reproducible in varying scales of operation.

The physical ramifications of the design are essentially non-contextual. That is the resultant of an inherent universality. But this is, in turn, the product of the very invisibility of the word. The container receives, stores, dispenses and exchanges the word. It is also a space to inspire new dreams, visions of many futures. In Wales, the 'dreamtime' has deep roots. Alsop intends to draw them outwards with just that degree of benign sorcery that the age demands.

Design objectives and approach

Various objectives were considered in order to fulfil the following design criteria within the clients budget. Those included: high environmental quality; low running cost, flexibility and adaptability, but good security; low-maintenance costs and sound quality control to be linked to low construction costs and phased construction. Subsequently, the phasing proved invaluable when Phase II, the library, was indefinitely postponed (April 1993).

To fulfil these objectives the design team had elevated the library to generate a secure enclosure above the ground. Beneath the library a sheltered public space was to be generated. The ground could be paved to follow the existing slope.

An environmental buffer zone had to be created around the building to minimise heat gain in summer and likewise heat loss in winter, and to provide an acoustic filter to the noisy external environment.

The building is designed to maximise the use of free energies, such as daylight, solar heat in the winter and solar ventilation in the summer; accompanied in the summer by night-time cooling , ground water cooling and wind to aid ventilation.

Structural principles

A repetitive structural system is being developed which may be easily adapted to

accommodate the changing needs of the client, such as extra floors, position of vertical risers, stairs, and light-wells as well as distribution of services.

The structural principles were also original in the context. The superstructure consists of standard *cubic* composite planar system having a panel size of 12 x 18 metres repetitive floor system, supported by perimeter and internal columns.

The floor system consists of a repetitive 1.2 metre deep cubic space frame with a reinforced concrete topping. To minimise the weight (and thus cost of steelwork) the concrete topping and the steel frame are to be designed to act compositely.

The space frame provides adequate depth for the distribution of ductwork and positioning of fan coil units.

The whole frame is clad in metal and glass. External movable shading devices are supported off aluminium brackets which are fixed to the primary frame.

The primary structure frame is fire-protected. Fire sprinklers are built-in as standard.

Stability is paramount. The superstructure is a 'braced table' on which the stiff library frame is erected.

As regards the substructure, *two* substructures have been considered.

Firstly, with a basement car park: the substructure will consist of a reinforced concrete frame. The substructures will be open on three sides to ensure adequate cross ventilation is maintained. Therefore, the need for mechanical ventilation systems will not be required. The basement raft slab will be founded on suitable bearing strata.

Secondly, a substructure without a basement car park was considered. In this case, the perimeter columns will be founded on strip foundations bearing on suitable strata. The ground floor will consist of paving tiles placed on suitable back fill.

Environmental principles

The building is designed to minimise

energy consumption by the use of efficient systems and free environmental energy, whilst creating a wide variety of spaces that are flexible in their use and adaptable to changing client demands.

The elevated library is serviced from a centralised plant room, which will supply heating, hot and cold water, electrical power and communication to all floors. Fan coil units (supply and extract) will be positioned within the structural floor depth and fresh air will be taken directly from outside. Air will be exhausted by utilising the fan coil unit with heat recovery in winter or by taking advantage of the stack effect and thermal draught created by the thermal flue.

External perimeter shading devices will provide solar control on the south, east and west elevations. Glare and daylight control will be provided by an internal blind on all facades including the north.

The perimeter buffer zone will reduce noise level from outside to within. All perimeter spaces are daylit. Activities that require less daylight will be positioned in the central zones.

Ventilation

Specific ventilation modes are designed for winter and summer. During the summer day, cool ground water is pumped to a heat exchanger on the roof which then cools water supplied to each fan coil unit. Fresh air is drawn directly from outside via the fan coil units, entering the room via a floor displacement system. When necessary the air is pre-cooled by the ground water system. External movable shades protect the building from excessive solar gain.

At night lunar coolers positioned on the roof radiate heat to the outer atmosphere. By doing so they themselves will become cooler than the outside air temperature and they can be used to cool the water which is then supplied directly to the fan coil units. The fans draw cool night-time air directly into the building, where it is circulated and is then ventilated out through the perimeter

thermal flue. As air is circulated it will cool down the structure, which then acts as a cool store to provide 'radiant' coolth to occupants during the heat of the day. The whole night-time operation will utilise low night-time electricity charges.

A different ventilation mode operates in the winter. During the day the roof solar collectors will be used to supplement the hot water supply to the fan coil units, to perimeter heating at each facade and to the toilet facilities. Minimum fresh air is supplied directly from outside via the fan coil units into the library space. The air is preheated as it passes through the fan coil units by a heat exchanger and is exhausted up the thermal flue, keeping the building warm. Warm air within the southern parts of the thermal flue will be drawn around to the cooler northern face of the building.

At night the building is closed and the perimeter buffer zone reduces heat loss. Fifty per cent of CO_2 emitted into the atmosphere is generated from servicing buildings.

The energy consumption of the development is minimised by maximising the use of free energies such as sun, ground-water cooling, and night-time cooling. Also, waste is minimised with the aid of the perimeter buffer zone and use of energy efficient equipment.

A high quality internal environment is being developed accordingly here for less than 50 per cent of the energy requirements of a traditional air-conditioned building.

Construction

Construction sequence was an important consideration in design, as well as speed of construction. The building is to be constructed in two phases:
– Phase I: 3260 square metres
– Phase II: 4400 square metres
Indeed the whole development may be constructed within less than 12 months.

In Phase I the complete superstructure is erected, but only the ground floor and first floor structure will be clad and fitted out for

use. When Phase II proceeds the fabric enclosing the second and third floors will be removed and the remaining floors fitted out as required by future needs. The plant room unit will be relocated to the roof level. In April 1993 it was decided not to proceed beyond Phase I.

With regard to overall costings, considerable new ground was broken in establishing economical criteria. Firstly, to those not familiar with putting Alsop's architecture into practice, the image that the building represents appears to be expensive. This is a misconception which construction cost consultants are keen to dismiss.

During the actual course of the competition, adjustments were made to the project budget which have necessitated reappraisals of the scheme to ensure its continued viability. Subsequently, it was possible to include costs relating to a wider range of potential project scopes and specifications.

The base scheme, which represents the architects' response to the original cost brief provided a prestigious, high quality facility with more area and uses than were strictly required. The cost of this scheme ranged from 13.9 to 14.5 million pounds depending on the phasing option chosen, these costs being inclusive of an underground car park.

Given that the budget was subsequently reduced from 14 million to 10.5 million pounds, potential changes were recommended which would reduce costs. Several ideas for cost reduction were considered which held to the basic concept originated by Will Alsop.

Project Team
Alsop & Störmer Architects: *Proj. Architect* William Alsop, *Assistants* Isabelle Lousada, Emmanuelle Poggi, *Lanscape Architect* Jenny Coe, *Model Maker* Unit 22; *Literary and Artistic Consultant*: Mel Gooding; *Engineer*: Ove Arup & Partners – *Service Eng.* Guy Battle, *Structural Eng.* Chris McCarthy; *Quantity Surveyor*: Hanscomb – Jonathan Harper, Danica Farren; *Struc. System Consultants and Computer Images*: ASW Cubic Structures; *Visuals*: John Camm; *Photographer*: Roderick Coyne

MEL GOODING

THE CELEBRATION OF THE WORD
SWANSEA

What is envisaged is a site for the celebration of the word in all its manifestations. A focal point at which energies will converge: energies historical, cultural, mythical, spiritual, philosophical, literary, rhetorical. A vocal point, a place of utterance, a place of making, and a place for the performance of the mysteries of the word, a place for graceful ceremony and for unaffected pleasures. An auditorium in the true sense: a place of hearing and listening; a sounding chamber resonating with the spoken word at its most magical and majestic.

It must be a place that remembers the specificities of Wales: the great mythic books that contain the matter of Wales, the branches of the Mabinogi, the tales and romances, the Black Book of Carmarthen and all; the bardic poetics of the Cynfeirdd, the epic pride and grief of the Gododdin; the infinite variety of the Cywdd and its greatest master Dafydd ap Gwilym; the great renaissance poets of Wales: Vaughan, Herbert and all their successors down to those of the modern renaissance of Welsh poetry in Welsh and English: W H Davies, Wilfred Owen, Saunders Lewis, Edward Thomas, Idries Davies, J Kitchener Davies, and Swansea's own Vernon Watkins; Dylan Thomas and John Ormond, and many more; the hymns of Pantycelyn and other masters; the vitalities of Welsh fiction and drama; language of the Chapel and Meeting House, of the authorised version heard by generations, of stupendous preachings and simple appeals to the heart always in the democratic vernaculars of Welsh or of Welsh English; the argumentation and rhetoric of union lodge and of the open hillsides where the union men and the political leaders spoke to the hard-working poor and articulated for them a vision of earthly dignity, the passionate cadences of Lloyd George, Aneurin Bevan and Neil Kinnock.

The National Centre and its museum must celebrate all the branches of that unique Welsh tradition in which the spoken word was and is central to the life and continuity of its languages and literatures: its design and the arrangements of its facilities must reflect this undeniable fact of Welsh cultural and literary history. These languages, morally inflected, poetic, were spiritually nourished by a thousand sermons, a thousand political speeches and addresses, by a knowledge received no less through the ear than the eye.

Neither must the Centre overlook the achievements of Welsh scholarship in linguistics and historiography, philosophy and theology. It will become a rich resource for the academic community of Wales and of the wider world: the development of the library and especially of the reference library, in Phase II, takes on a particular significance in this light. The library is integral to the proposal.

Ty Llen (literally, a house of literature) will be a place for writing as well as for reading; speaking as well as listening. The International Writers' Centre is thus at the heart of the proposal. The National Centre must be dynamically related to the international literary and scholarly community: by proudly proclaiming its Welsh identity it locates itself authentically as a sounding chamber for all literatures; a place with greatness to offer those who bring in exchange their own talents in other tongues.

Swansea is wonderfully placed to make this dynamic exchange: *Ty Llen* will be situated at the centre of a lively town coming once again into its own; a town that has long looked outward, a place of work and manufacture, a market for the produce of the land and of the sea, a trading place, a port, a place of recreation.

Like a shell by the great bay it will reverberate with the sound of the world's words.

Design objectives and approach

There was a definite feeling as the architectural concept developed that, as such, a Museum of the Word is both intriguing and infuriating as a title for the project. Intriguing because it contained all the ambiguity that would permit dreams to become visible. Infuriating because the very idea of the 'word' rests on its invisibility.

The urban context was seen as critical from the inception of the project.

The site is clearly at the western edge of the town centre. The other side of Dillwyn Street is of a different character. The western side of the town centre seems forgotten and in spite of the theatre, there is no anchor point to pull people through the town towards this edge. The development of parking facilities associated with the shopping centre has tended to create a centre of gravity to the west and south-west of the site. The potential development of the city centre falls into three areas; in close relation to each other.

Firstly, 'The Head':
This area to the east containing the theatre, Museum of the Word, the library, small scale shops, eating and drinking facilities.

Secondly, 'The Body':
This area focuses on the market and gathers other shops around it. All things necessary to physical well being are available here.

Thirdly, 'The Soul':
This area is focused on St Mary's Church

and the Castle Green Garden. (A combination of spiritual and historical reflection.)

As can be seen, the 'Head' lacks focus and it is through this simple analysis that ways of creating both a facility for the Museum of the Word and a focus, now emerged.

In fact, two squares emerge, for the whole site is envisaged as a public space and is thus divided into two squares.

Square I lies between the proposal building and the Grand Theatre. This square acts as a gateway for the western approach to the town centre. It acts as a gathering place that could be programmed with events in the summer. A partial roof over the space not only acts as a sun-shade for the library but also helps to contain the space and therefore define it.

Square II is under the building. It is more enclosed (for wind protection), but allows people to see Oxford Street. It seems important to visually unite Oxford Street and Singleton Street to work together to form the Western Gateway. Elements from the brief animate this square. Here are located the restaurant, café, wine bar, bookshop, International Writers' Centre and temporary exhibition. This mini city acts as a focus to the Western Gateway. The two squares both compliment and contrast with each other giving rise to an extraordinary situation, possibly one that is unique today.

Certain key considerations characterise the building. The idea was generated primarily by urban design considerations. Of paramount importance is the early completion of the ground level in Phase I. This part of town had suffered because of the parking lot and air of uncertainty consequently engendered. Phase II is constructed on top of Phase I.

For these reasons the bulk of the accommodation is to be housed in an elegant glass box over the public square. The box is constructed with a minimum of internal columns and employs energy-saving concepts. For example, a double-skin of glass creates a buffer zone which is able to save energy as well as contributing to noise reduction.

The link between the public square, museum and library is the bookshop. It will be possible to ride up in the lifts and to visit one or both of the facilities, then walk down a gentle ramp edged with bookshelves. The design allows the bookshop to maintain independent hours if required, and consequently a visitor will be able to browse freely and then purchase a book at ground level as required.

There are three distinct levels to the Glass Box: the first of these is the Museum of the Word.

The floor could contain strips of different experiences. On leaving the bookshop (entrance) a series of suspended forms can be sat in which contain pure light. In such an environment there is no perceived dimension. Inside is received the spoken word (a strong tradition in South Wales); also in this strip there are comfortable chairs with interactive screens, readily accessible.

The next strip is a more traditional form of glass cabinet in which valuable items can be shown. This strip has a glass floor which allows glimpses of its contents from the square below.

The following strip contains larger sound environments for words and images. These are contained within fluid spaces.

The fourth strip consists of parallel walls for conventional displays. The space inside these can be used as a store if need be.

The last strip contains shelves of books for reference together with computer teminals, comfortable chairs and domestic quality light. This area is seen as a facilitator to an individual enquiry into the Word, providing opportunity and potential.

Fundamentally, the whole floor is a resource; a resource to be used, that is. By definition this becomes, inherently, a repository for the prose, poetry and matter of Wales.

The two floors above the museum originally contain Phase II which is the public library, with all its constituent parts. This may now be shelved.

For Phase I the 'roof' space would be covered with a temporary fabric weather shield which would allow the space to be used for events.

The libraries contain space and light. Although these are air-temperature controlled, the windows can be opened for the buffer zone which allows air to be partially filtered, thereby minimising the introduction of dirt into the space. The libraries are very flexible and can be rearranged to suit new ideas in the future. Working spaces exist on the building perimeter where there is good natural light and views. Like the Museum of the Word, the library brief must be developed.

The eventual roof space on top of Phase I in the library was considered here to be most important and to be used in such a way that would take advantage of the splendid views. Access is via the bookshop. On the roof a performance platform, a story-telling bush (a structure to be crawled into) and a garden were considered appropriate.

The garden is called the Garden of the World. Here the idea is to illuminate basic themes of the world – water, fire, skies, animal, earth etc – as represented in all languages and having a common root. The garden, which could be open to the skies, contains some representation of the constellations, stars, moon, sun. It is a place for story-telling. It could also provide the opportunity to name parts of the landscape such as hills, rocks and rivers.

This will be a place to be.

We see the whole ensemble as representative of a multiplicity of means of access to the world of the word.

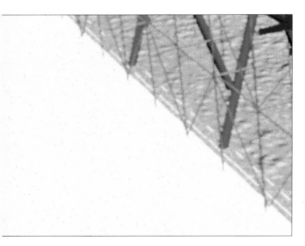

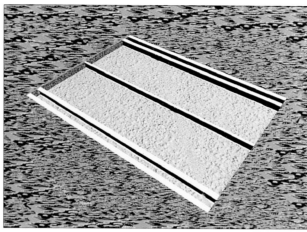
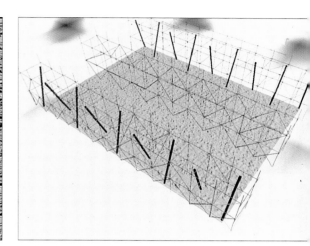
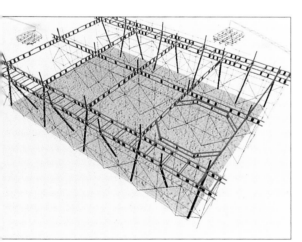
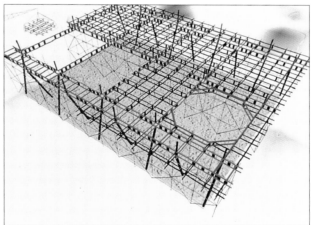
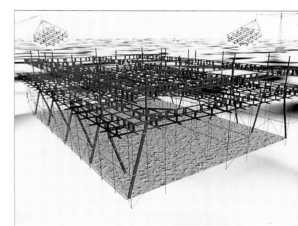

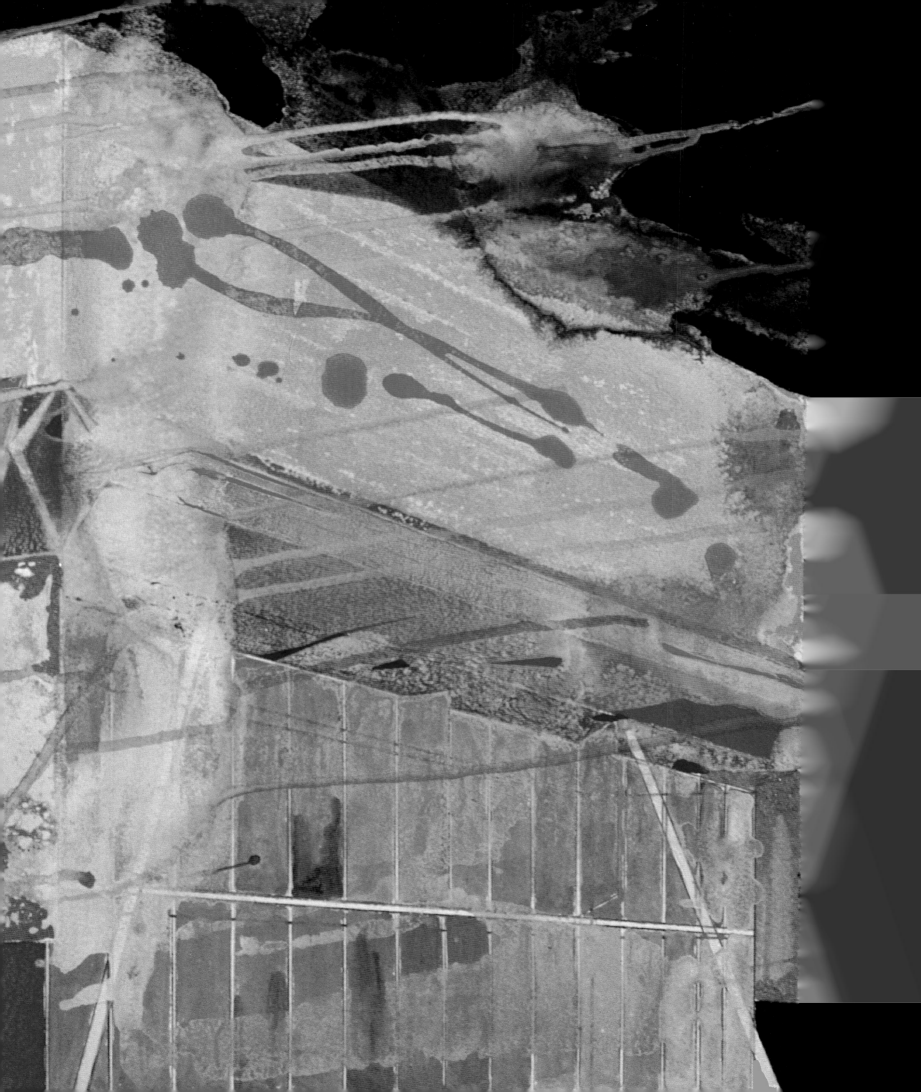

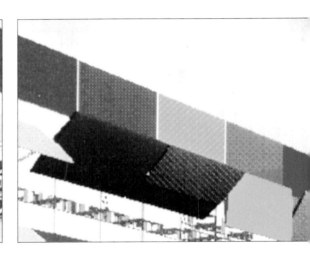
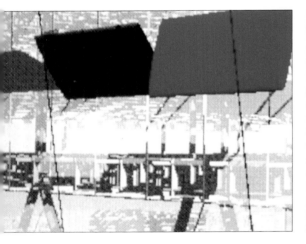

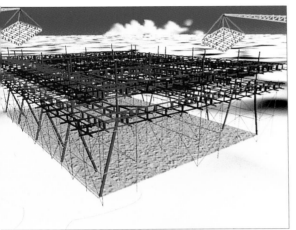
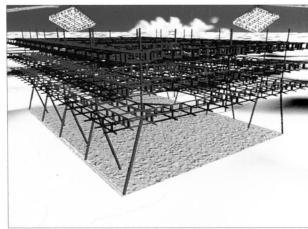
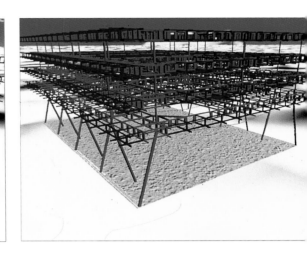
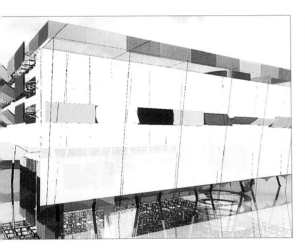

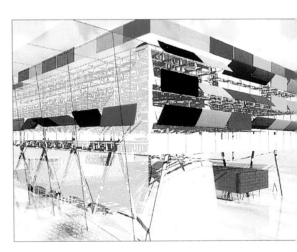

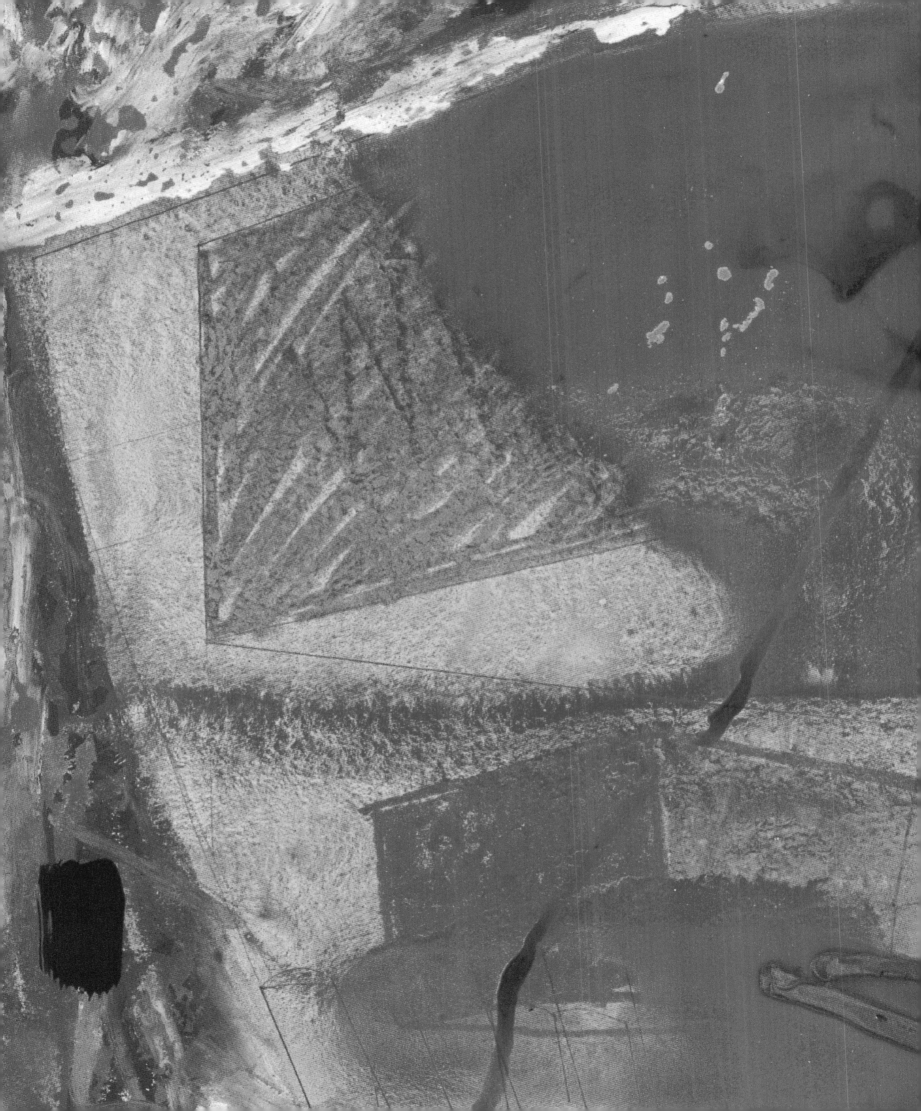

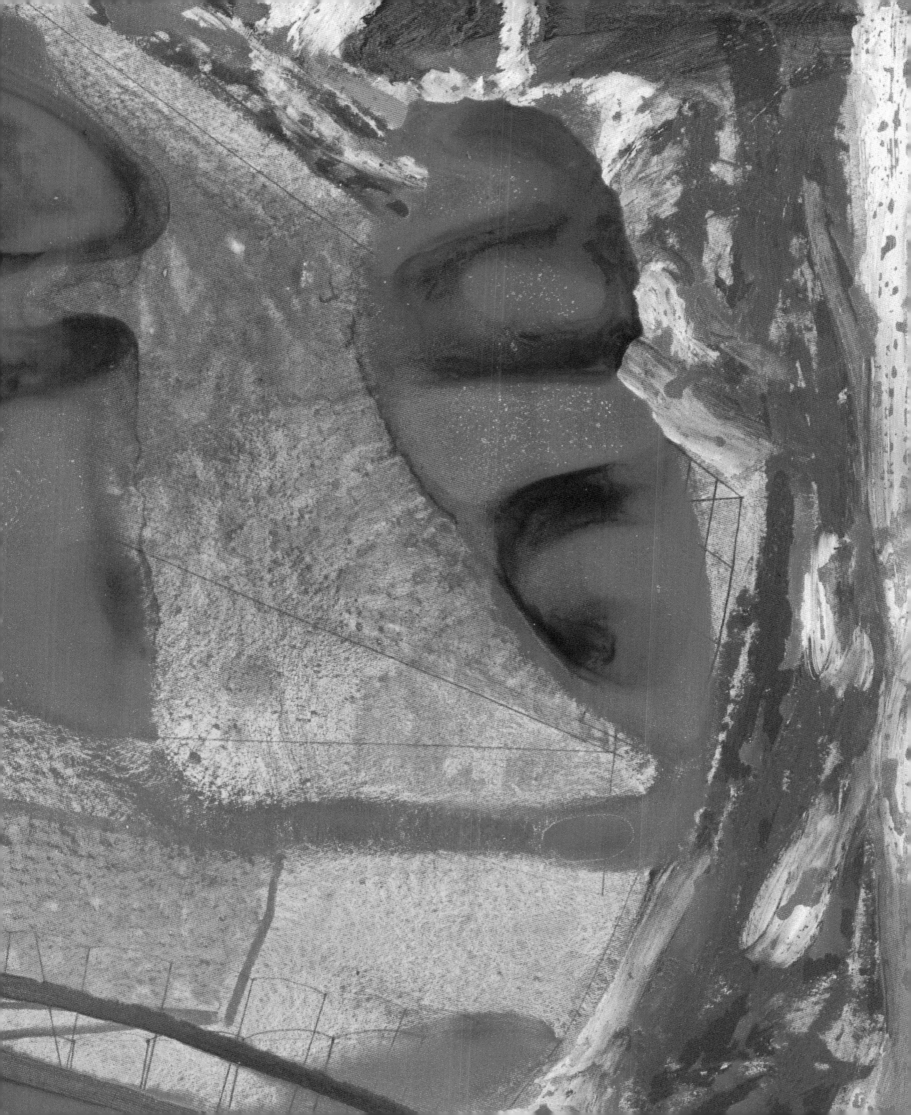

 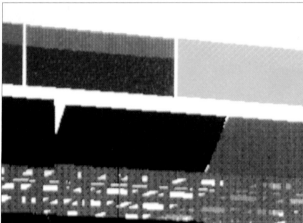 

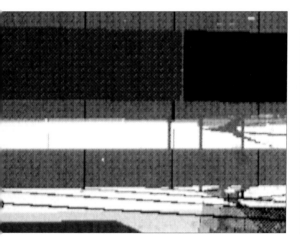  

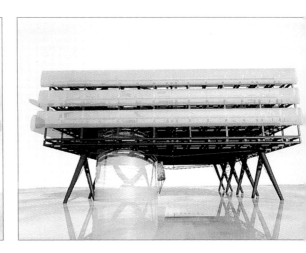

Opposite: Site plan; Roof level plan + 23.50m

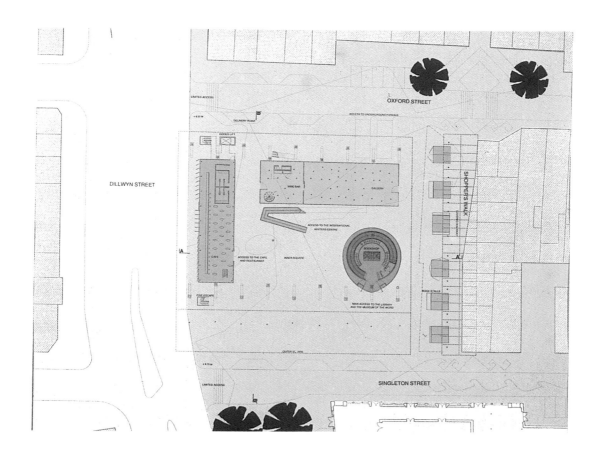

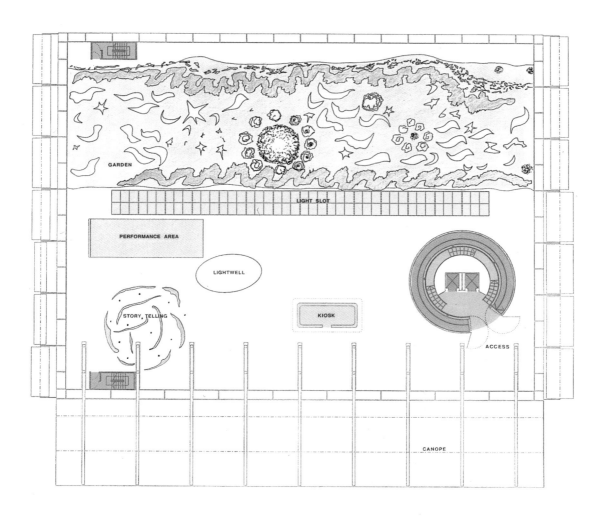

Opposite: Libraries, third floor plan +19.80m; Libraries, second floor plan +16.10m

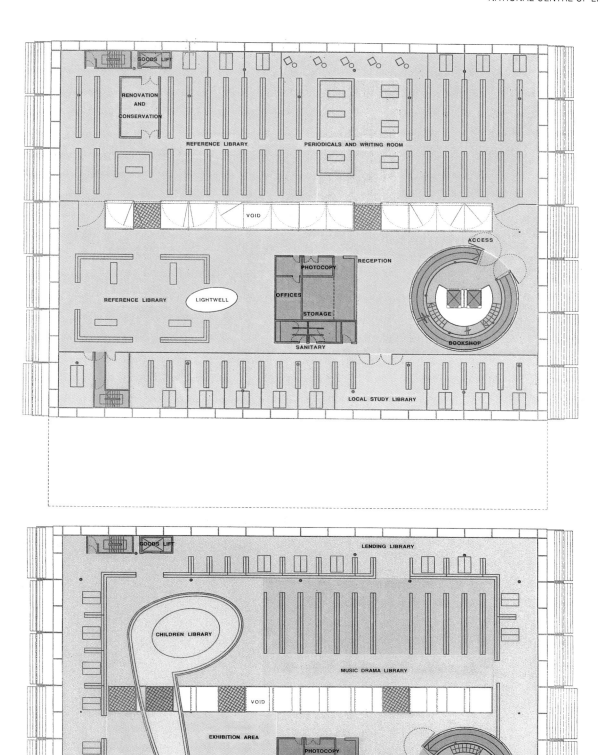

Opposite: Museum of the Word, first floor plan +12.40m; Level + 3.80m

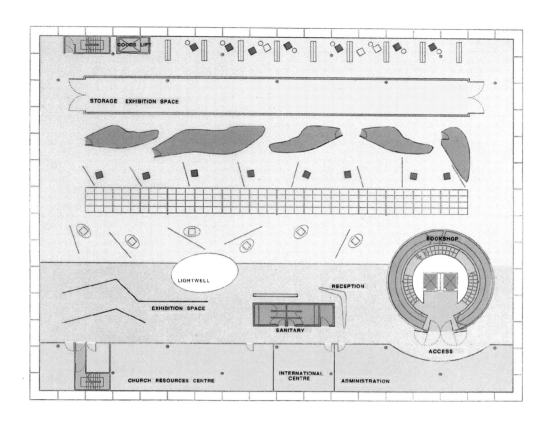

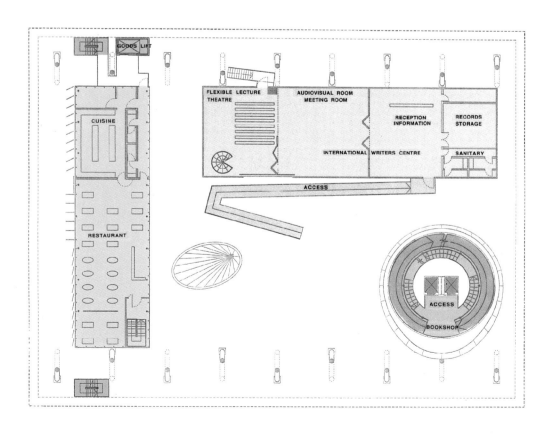

Opposite: North elevation; South elevation

Opposite: East elevation; West elevation

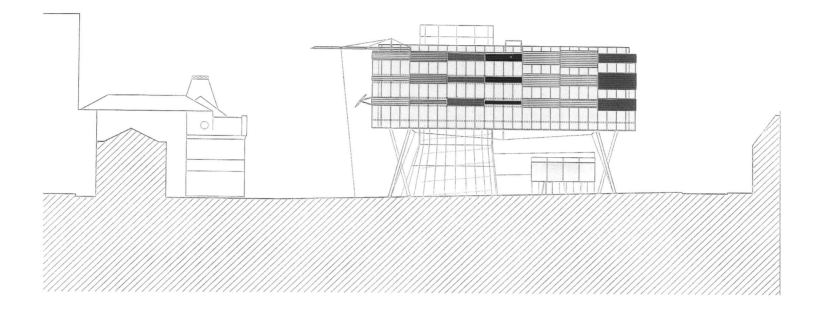

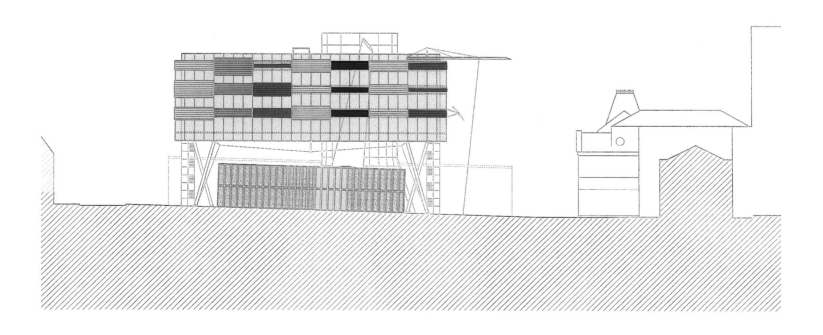

Opposite: Longitudinal section; Cross section

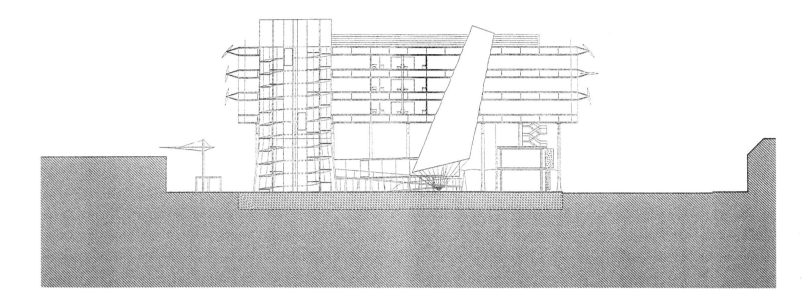

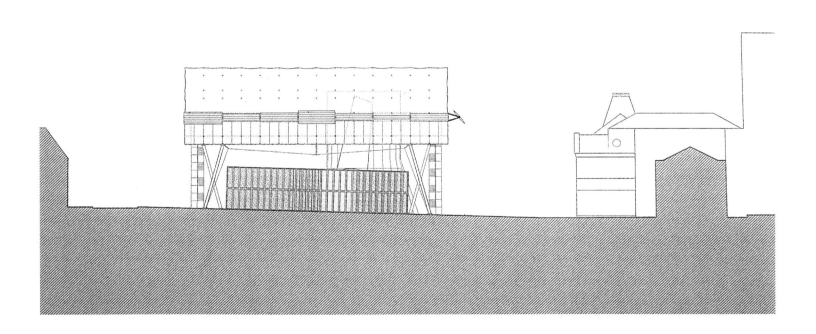

Opposite: Cross sections of structural details

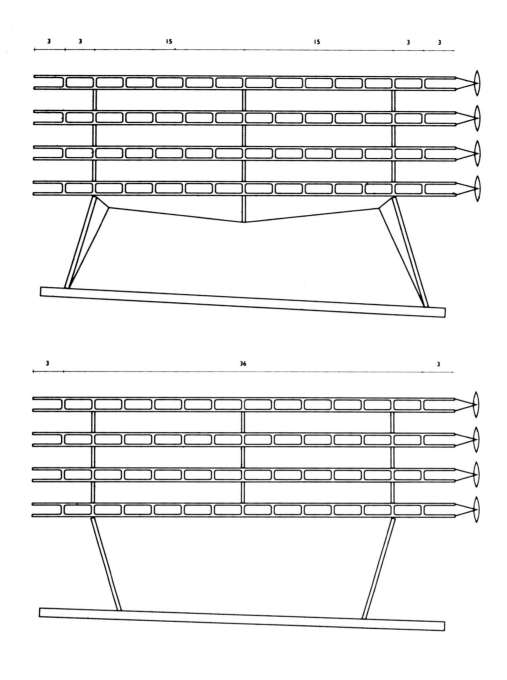

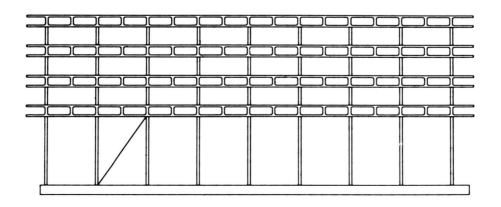

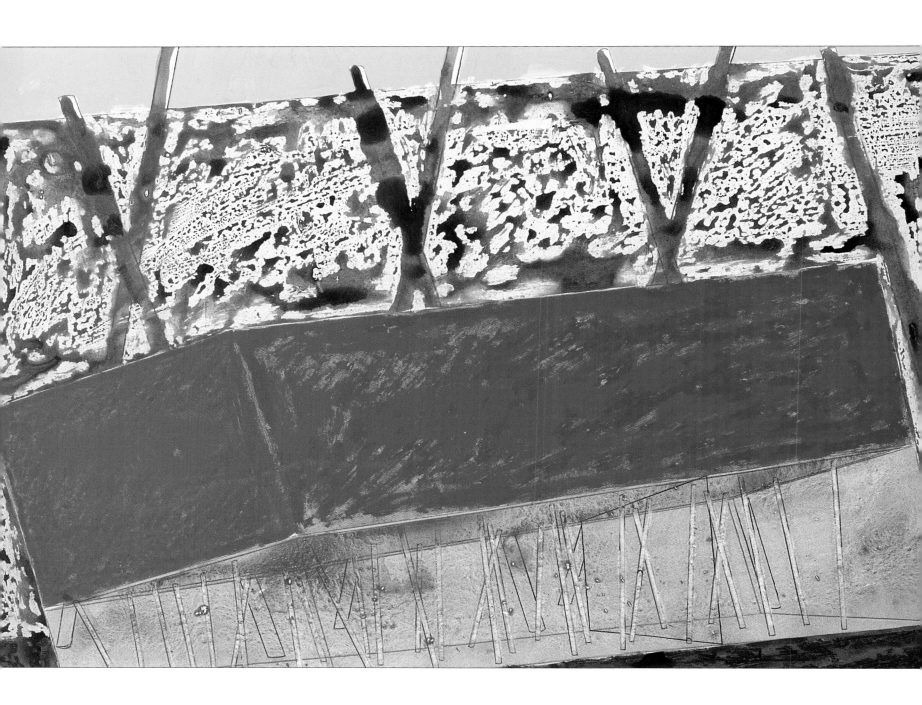

Opposite: Cross section structural detail; Longitudinal section structural detail; Typical library floor

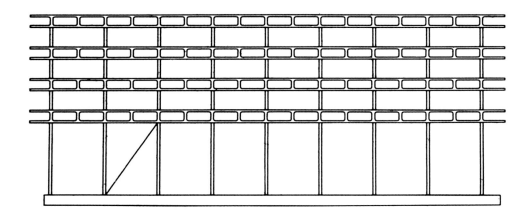

12m

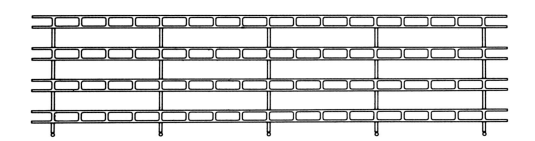

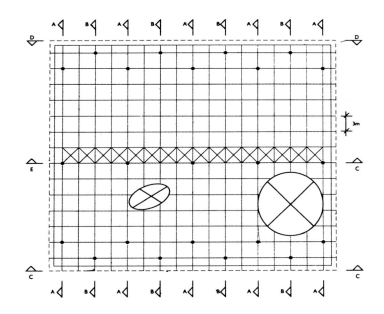

Opposite: Energy-saving targets; Environmental buffer zones; Construction and development

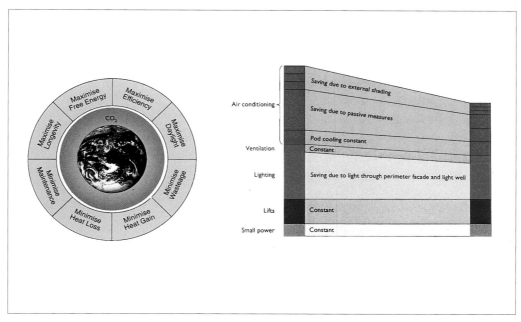

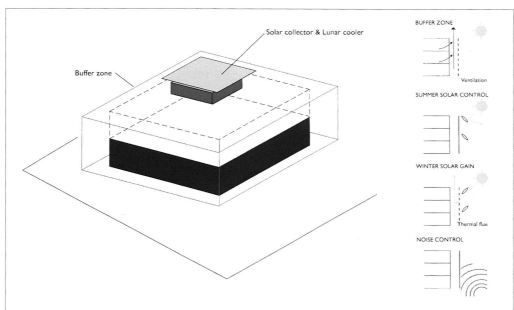

Solar collector & Lunar cooler

Buffer zone

BUFFER ZONE

Ventilation

SUMMER SOLAR CONTROL

WINTER SOLAR GAIN

Thermal flue

NOISE CONTROL

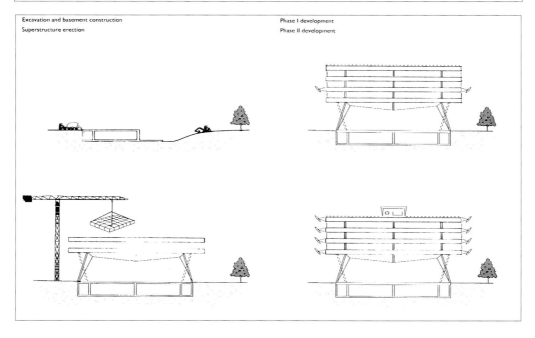

Excavation and basement construction

Superstructure erection

Phase I development

Phase II development

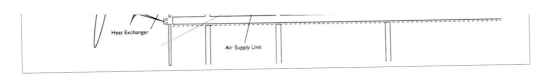

Heat Exchanger

Air Supply Unit

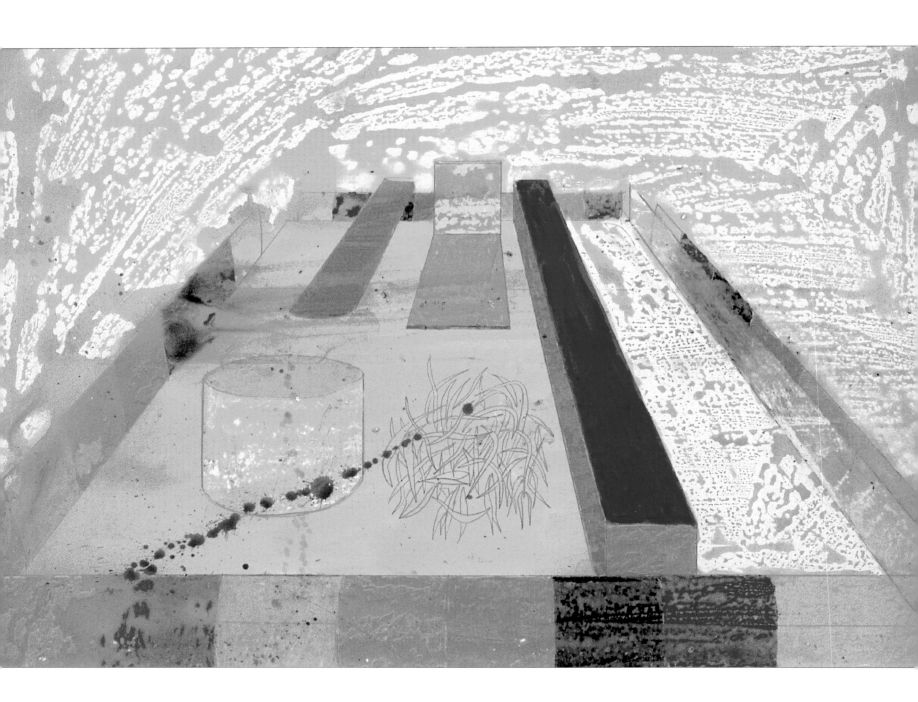

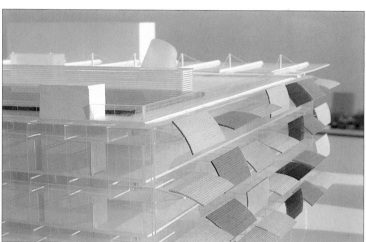

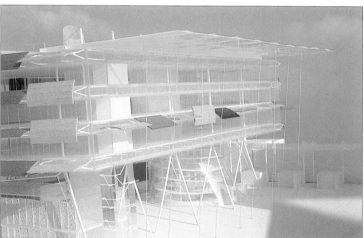

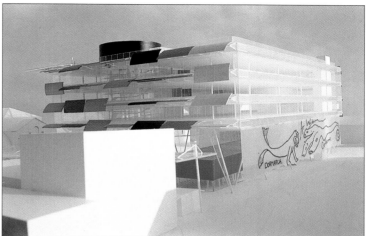

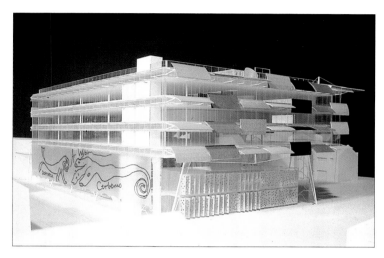

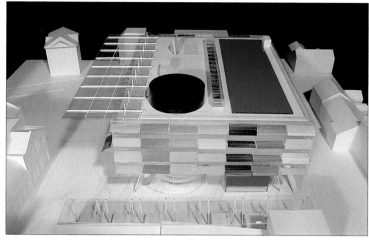

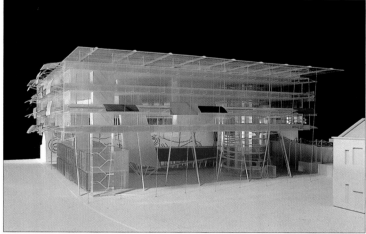

HOLGER JAEDICKE, CHRIS McCARTHY AND GUY BATTLE

THE WORLD TRADE CENTRE NUREMBERG

In the autumn of 1992, the city of Nuremberg organised an invited competition with the aim to develop a site at the periphery of the city centre.

The project in this central location near Nuremberg's main station was challenging in many ways. The brief had to be developed in the three stages of the competition in discussion with the city and the developer. The only essential requirement was to keep the existing coach station in some form on the site. The surrounding urban situation had evolved rather accidentally after the dereliction caused by the destruction during the Second World War. The adjacent 'Marienplatz' did not possess any defined quality with regard to design or usage of the surrounding buildings; it was thus appropriate for redevelopment.

To resolve the first stage it was proposed that a mixed development should be organised in two buildings. The entrance to the elevated cinema complex above the coach station was linked to a public shopping concourse in the main block. This concourse offered an attractive route for pedestrians connecting the city quarter around the Marienplatz with the main station. The functions in the high-rise block were organised in horizontal layers: two-storey basement parking, coach station on street level, shops on ground and first floor, four-storey offices and a three-storey high quality boarding house at the top.

The concept for the coach station was to provide a clear layout for easy use in conjunction with an entertaining environment for the passengers; thereby avoiding the sinister atmosphere usually pervading such facilities.

With the Marienplatz now cleared from all car traffic, the remaining gap in the perimeter closed by the restrained facade of the new development, uses typical design elements of urban squares to create a kind atmosphere for relaxation in the city. It can also be utilised for temporary events.

In the subsequent scheme development, the cinema idea was dropped in favour of a more substantial office development in the form of a World Trade Centre Organisation. While the concept of the mixed development was kept, it took the shape of two parallel buildings which are connected by a large public atrium for shopping and exhibition use. Securing the idea of creating a lively place in the city fabric, this oriented to both the newly designed square and the main station.

Attention was also directed towards a design that would be energy efficient by exploiting the performance of buffer zones, solar shadings and the thermal mass of the structure.

The building is clad in glass, but a range of different types were proposed according to the varying performance required.
Holger Jaedicke

Buildings consume 50 per cent of Europe's energy and are responsible for 50 per cent of Europe's carbon-dioxide production. The European Community acknowledges this fact and has laid out new low energy directives which describe the need to minimise the use of primary energy by maximising efficiency and maximum use of renewable energy sources; for example, solar energy for heating and power supply, wind for ventilation and power, daylight for lighting; and the utilisation of the inherent benefits with regard to materials, such as insulation to reduce heat loss and thermal mass to negate the need for air conditioning.

The new Alsop & Störmer scheme for Nuremberg embraces these directives and aims to take them even further.

Nuremberg is an environmentally friendly building, developed through an engineering understanding of the interaction of structure and materials with climatic forces in architecture.

The following have been achieved:
– A narrow plan and central atrium permit all offices to be daylit. In combination with a sensitive artificial lighting control system this will lead to a significant reduction in energy consumption – up to 60 per cent for lighting
– A central atrium permits stack effect cross ventilation during all periods of the year. This, in combination with an exposed concrete floor slab in each of the offices, will negate the need for any mechanical ventilation or cooling, apart from the warmest and coldest periods of the year
– Ventilated hollow-core slabs give access to the thermal mass in the centre of each floor slab, permitting them to be used to store the heat during the winter months and the cool in the summer
– Variable shading on all external facades allows satisfactory control of glare and solar energy in the summer and permits maximum use of direct solar heating during the winter.

The EEC has set an environmental energy standard. This building goes beyond that standard and will be considered for EEC funding under the Thermie programme.
Chris McCarthy and Guy Battle

Project Team
Alsop & Störmer Architects: William Alsop, Jan Störmer, Holger Jaedicke; *Computer Images:* Benny O'Looney and Stephen Bedford

Scheme I

Scheme III

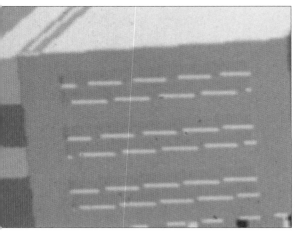

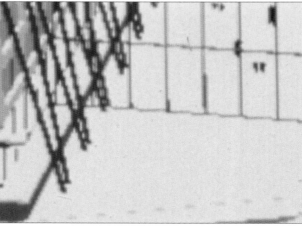

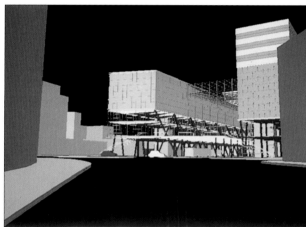
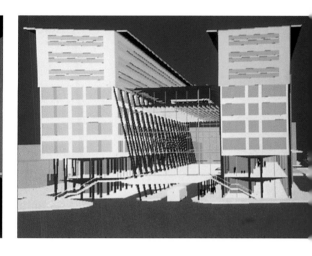
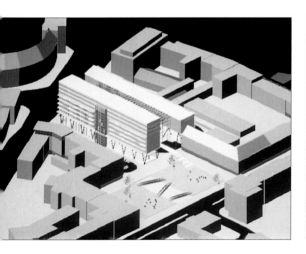
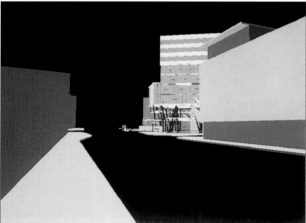

Scheme IV

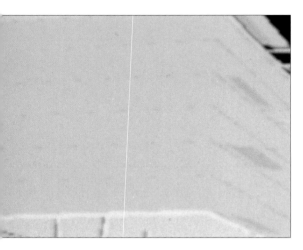

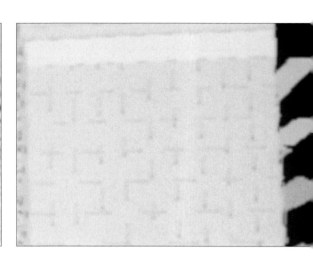

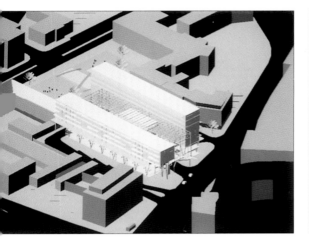

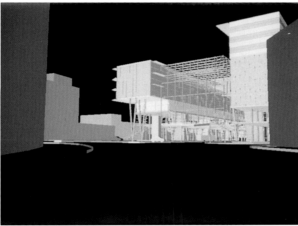

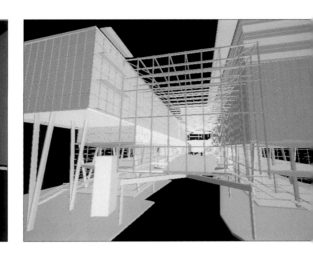

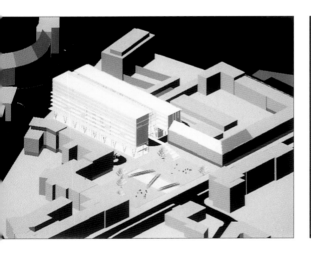

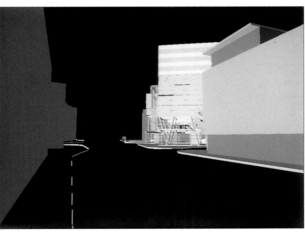

Opposite: Site plan; Sixth to eighth floor plan

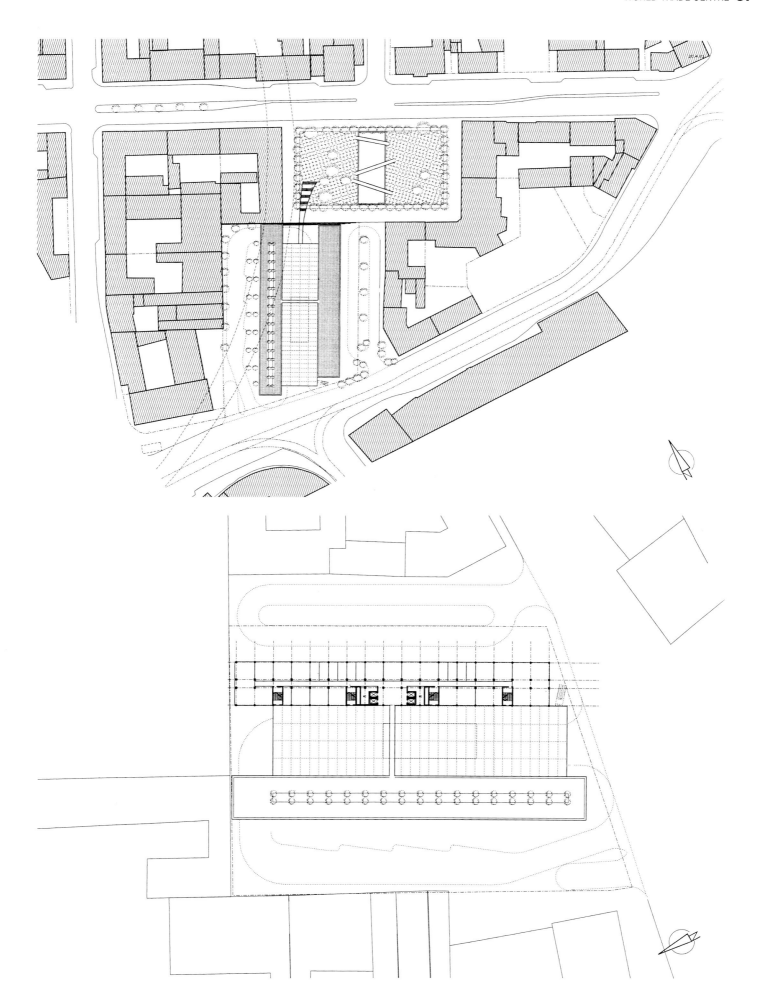

Opposite: Third to fifth floor plan; Second floor plan

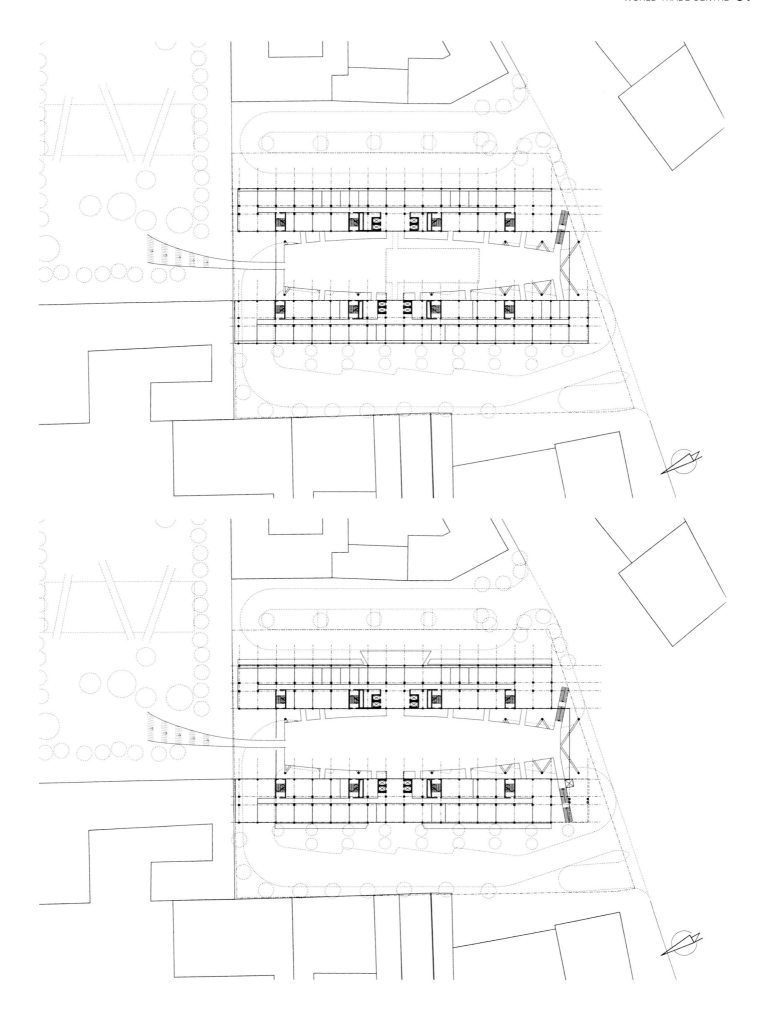

Opposite: First floor plan; Ground floor plan

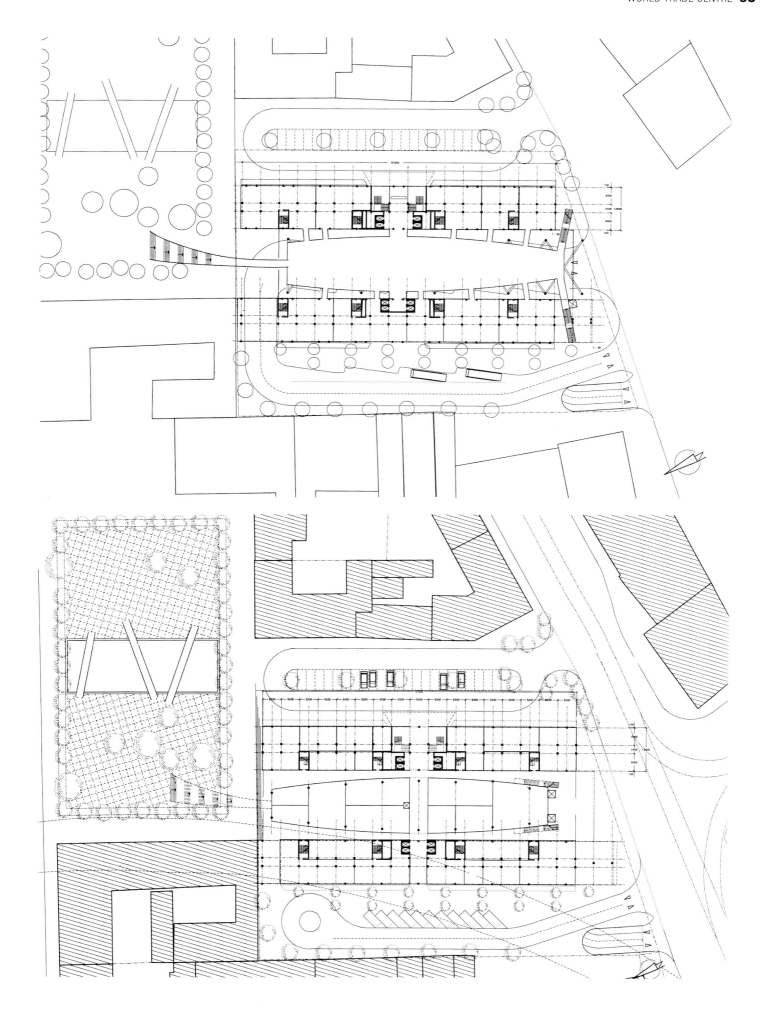

Opposite: Street level plan; First basement floor plan

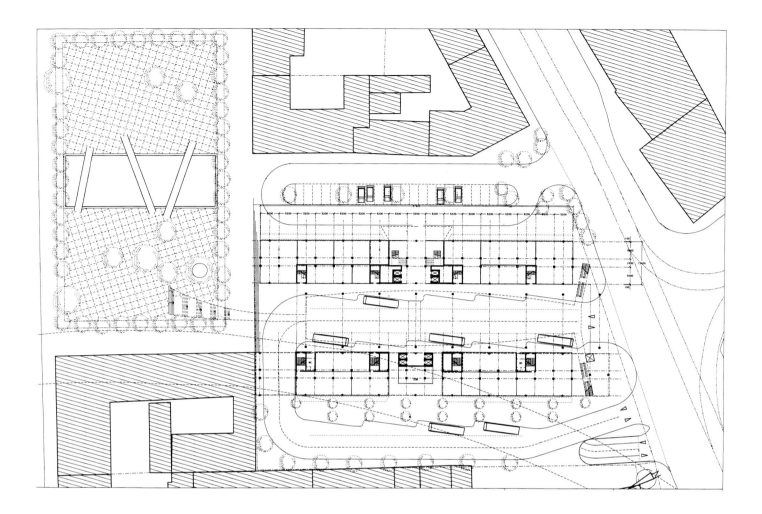

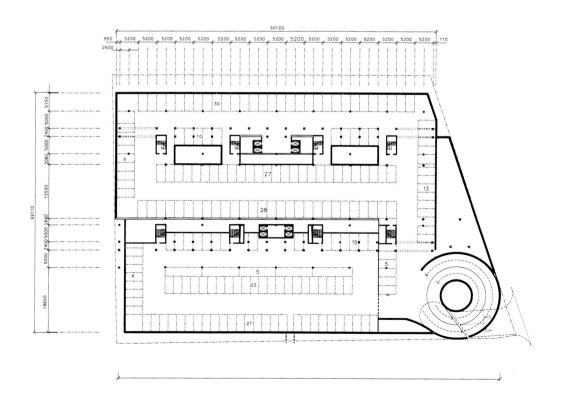

Opposite: Cross section; North elevation; East elevation; Longitudinal section through atrium

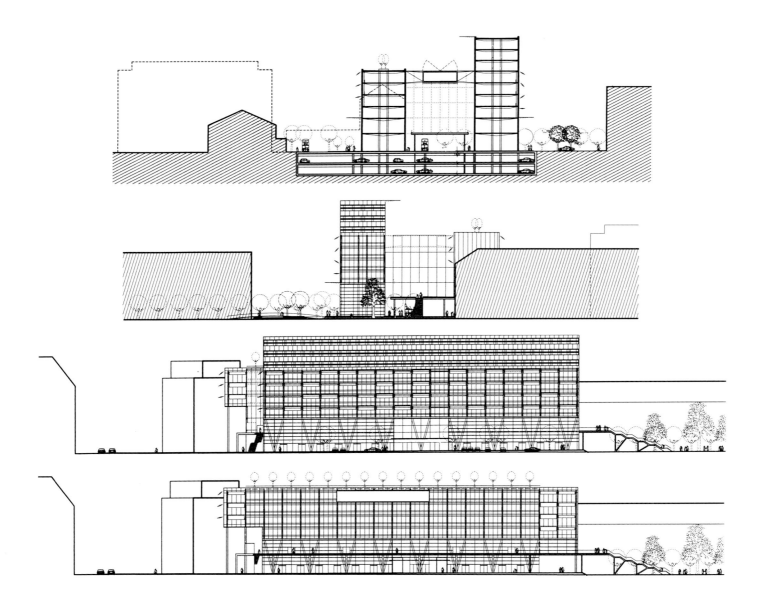

MICHAEL SPENS

KAUFHAUS DES NORDENS HAMBURG

The department store project is so designed as to unite opposites; the mutual antipathy of two department stores as Alsop was invited to reverse seemed irrevocable. The older of the two buildings was listed; the younger totally destroying any environmental character offered by the former. There was, furthermore, little real attraction to the passing motorists to pull off the distributor route. Alsop immediately set about creating a positive magnet out of the younger building, while linking this with the new version by a series of bridges crossing an atrium. The most pronounced aspect of this magnet was to be the glowing horizontal symbol in rainbow colours. The long street facade, first observed from the primary distributor road, became by contrast completely opaque. This concept appears at an early stage in the developmental paintings relating to this project.

Design objectives

The two existing buildings were to be combined into a single shopping experience while ensuring that the views through Lange Mühren Street would remain as unrestricted as possible. A new department store image was required which would be different when the store was open and when it was closed.

Daylight was to be allowed to enter the basement level. Car parking was to be maximised on the Horten site in order to liberate the Kaufhof parkhouse.

The listed building, Kaufhof, it was felt should not be touched in any way by the new face of the Horten Store.

The problem of combining the former in a single image with a refurbished existing building is resolved by combining the glass aesthetic of the cover to the street with the

new image of Horten. The single glass structure stands as a crystal alongside yet part of Kaufhof. This is achieved by minimising the structure for the roof.

Alsop & Störmer proposed two different solutions combined into one building:
– the facade onto Mönckebergstrasse is seen as a shop window. At ground level it is envisaged that the shop floor can be seen as a stage-set with the lighting of specific objects leading the eye into the shop
– the facade to Steintorwall is double glass (buffer zone). This is seen as a large shop window which can be enlivened by electronic images/messages or actual objects. What you see is a shop, not a building.

In the day the shop is seen as a composition of different types of colourless glass. At night when the store is closed it is proposed that the building will be coloured with light. The building becomes a beacon at the gateway to Mönckebergstrasse and a point of interest as the wall to Steintorwall

The street level of Lange Mühren is completely removed and replaced by a narrow glass block 'bridge'. This allows the daylight to penetrate the basement level which increases the value of this continuous floor space.

Two new parking decks to the Horten building were proposed. Which, with the ramp, will allow 672 spaces in one car park and therefore avoid the confusion of two different parkhouses. The necessity for a car bridge above the road is also removed. The Kaufhof car park could be demolished and rebuilt with a new function such as a shop or office.

The new structure does not touch the Kaufhof building. The roof is cantilevered from Horten and the end walls to Lange Mühren Street are stopped ten-centimetres

short of the listed building. This is of considerable significance.

New lighting systems were of critical importance in the design.

An Active Display Panel (ADP) was employed to create an active screen to be used as a glazing system made of multisection glass panels. These ADP panels will be manufactured from 'obscuraview' laminated into a 2 x 4 millimetre glass framework of anodised aluminium, incorporating a facility for the active screen to be switched on and off (opaque to clear and vice versa).

Conventional external cladding systems have fixed properties in terms of their acoustic, thermal and solar performance. Although designers endeavour to optimise these properties they operate inefficiently for much of the year due to their static nature.

By incorporating ADP in a double glazed unit an 'adaptive' facade can be produced. In doing so the facade will respond automatically to the external environment by altering its properties to maintain optimum internal conditions.

The benefit of this is that by reducing internal heat build-up caused by solar gain in the summer, the cooling load on the central plant is reduced, and vice versa in winter time. Although the facade would provide shading, preventing glare, it will allow enough natural light to reduce the need for supplementary artificial light.

Structural concept

The conceptual link between the two existing department stores implies the design of an integral glazed roof over the street space and between the two buildings.

By considering the listed Kauhof building, the climate-moderating envelope has been developed as a cantilevered structure.

The span of 20 metres combined with a design for a light-flooded space implied a light-weight structure. To achieve this the composite system is proposed which uses the horizontal plans as stress-taking elements. Following detailed analysis the use of composite panels made from glass and polycarbonate is suggested. The glass on the outer faces gives good protection against weathering and normal abrasive wear and the polycarbonate core (usually used for bullet-proof glazing) is utilised structurally.

The polycarbonate is maintained at a working stress below its elastic creep limit of 14 Newton square metres.

The transparent panels are connected together by a metal frame through which continuous steel cables created an homogeneous stress transferring element. By the continuous linking of the panels in two directions a large cantilevering frame of high stiffness, transparency and high thermal insulation properties is created.

Due to the 20-metre cantilever, high stresses are built up which the existing Horten building would not be able to withstand without complex additional stiffening. Consistent with the reorganised circulation to the entrance area a series of integral frames is arranged along Lange Mühren, resolving all these forces without substantial alteration of the Horten structure.

These frames are made from prefabricated horizontal vierendeel beams connected by cast in brackets. Each vierendeel beam rests on storey-high columns which are on the street side and are primarily compression members. On the building (Horten) side tension forces are resolved by the use of tension members, until the increasing dead load reverses them to compression elements.

The whole structure is designed from prefabricated parts, resulting in a site erection time, and minimising site costs.

Existing services

– Proposed alterations do not affect the existing primary plant in either building
– Unified quality standard between buildings should be a goal
– Extensions to systems to extended areas will not fundamentally affect the existing infrastructure with the exception of a new power supplier to escalators
– Further investigations into the existing systems need to be carried out before any upgradings of refurbishment that may be required can be commented on.

Covered street

– A buffer zone is provided at street level for pedestrians
– Protection from wind, rain and snow is offered
– Reduction in wind chill and provision of shelter remove the psychological obstacle to the free movement of people between stores
– Heat extracted from the central areas of the stores could be used to provide background heating
– The roof contributes positively to reducing the energy consumption of the adjoining buildings.

Project Team
Alsop & Störmer Architects: William Alsop, Jan Störmer, Chris Eisner, Isabelle Lousada, Ludwig Meyer, Emanuelle Poggi, Martin Schneider; *Structural Engineering,* Atelier One: Neil Thomas, Schaich, Bergemann & Partners; *Service Engineering,* Atelier Ten: Patrick Bellew; *Quantity Surveying*: Hanscomb – Jonathan Harper, Mike Staples; *Lighting Design*: ILC – Michael Zandi; *Model Maker*: Tony Reason; *Computer Images:* Benny O'Looney

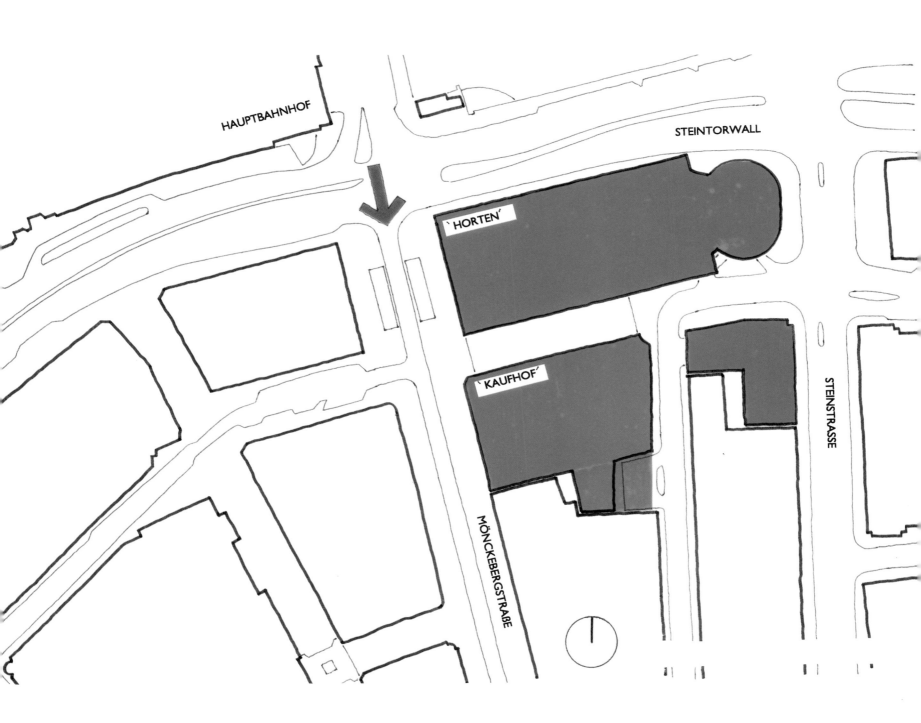

HAUPTBAHNHOF

STEINTORWALL

`HORTEN´

`KAUFHOF´

MÖNCKEBERGSTRAßE

STEINSTRASSE

Site plan

IF TONIGHT'S GAME

Trade

ES INTO EXTRA INNIN

JETZTZEIT

BEHUED NICELY

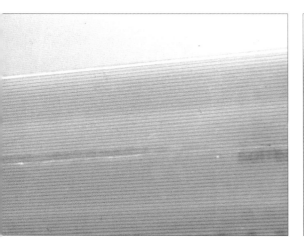
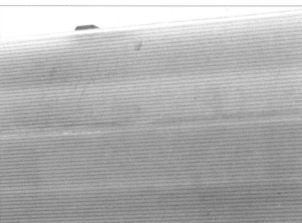

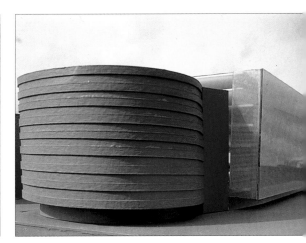

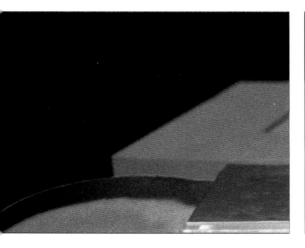

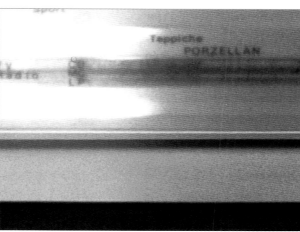

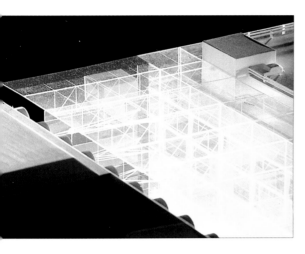
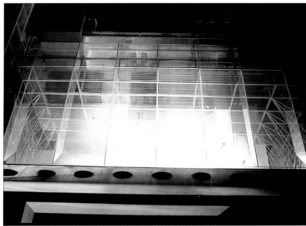
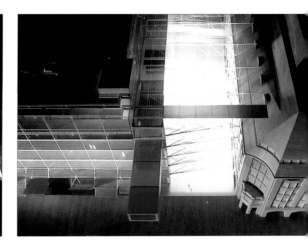

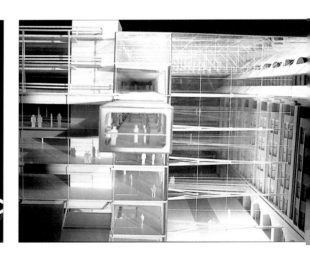

sport

Art through Technology

KÖRPER   ME

KAUFHAUS DES

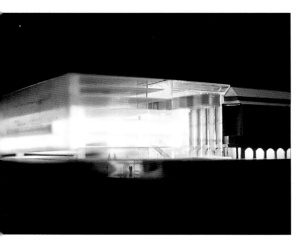

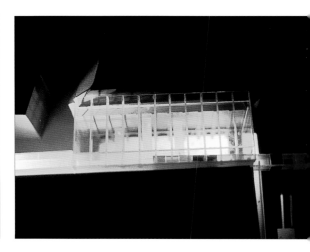

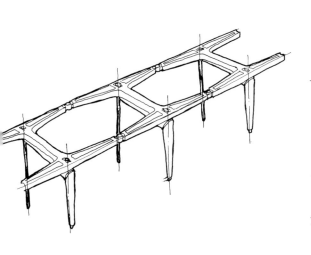
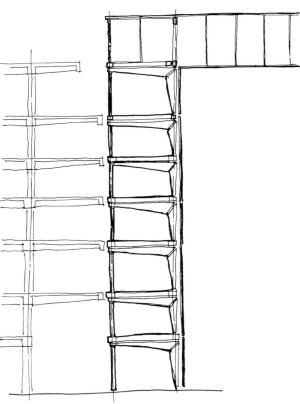
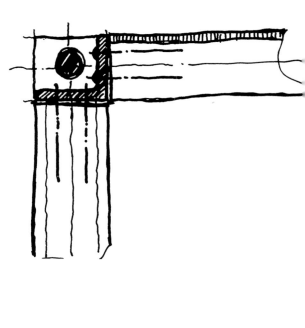

Axonometric detail of main structure   Section detail, main structure   Section detail of service duct within structure

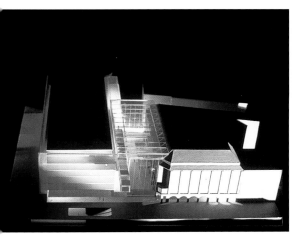

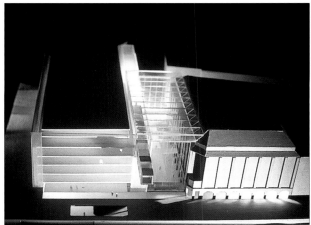

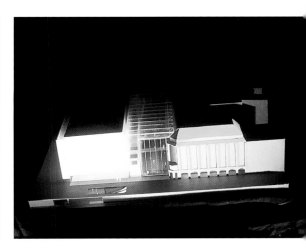

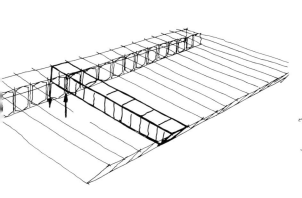

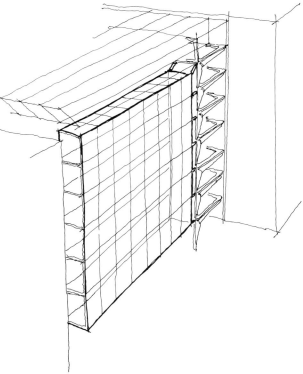

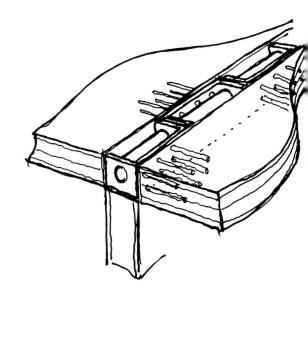

Axonometric detail of glass roof

Axonometric detail of glass endwall

Axonometric detail of service duct within structure

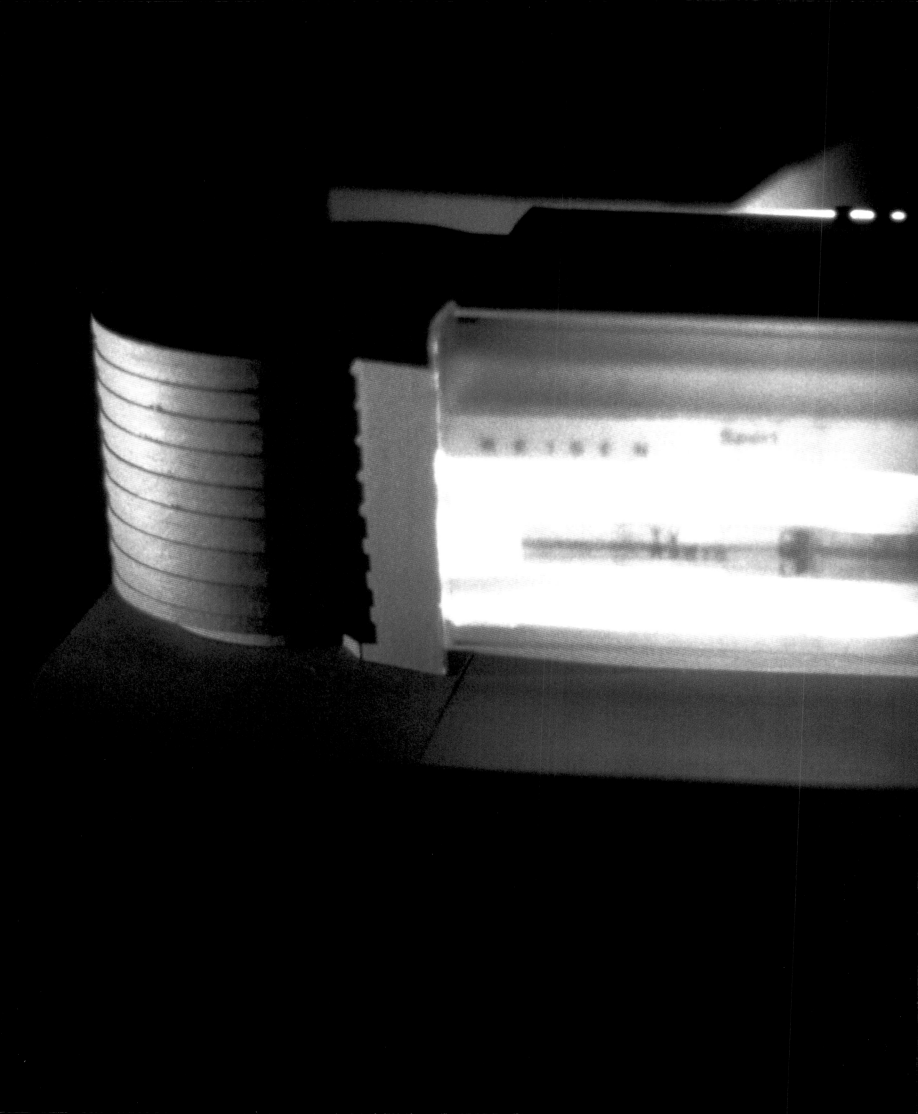

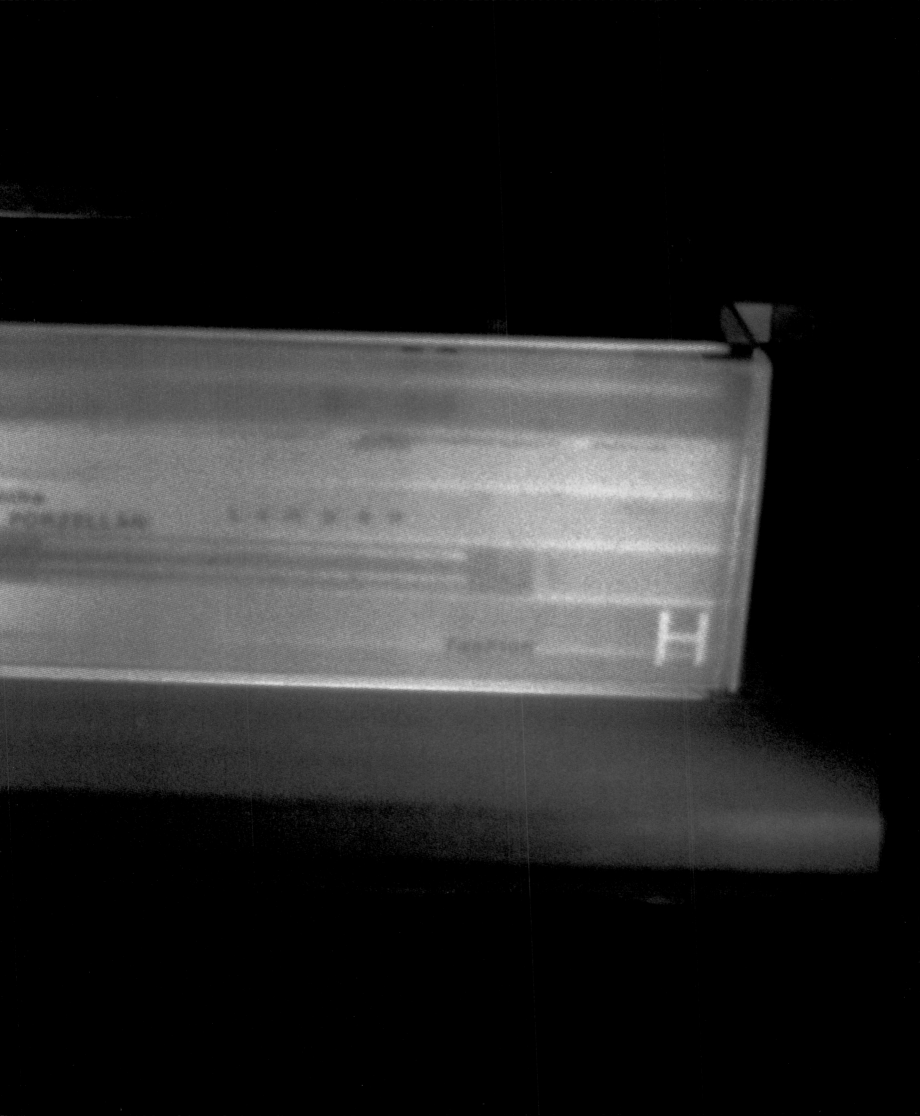

Opposite: Roof plan; Level four floor plan

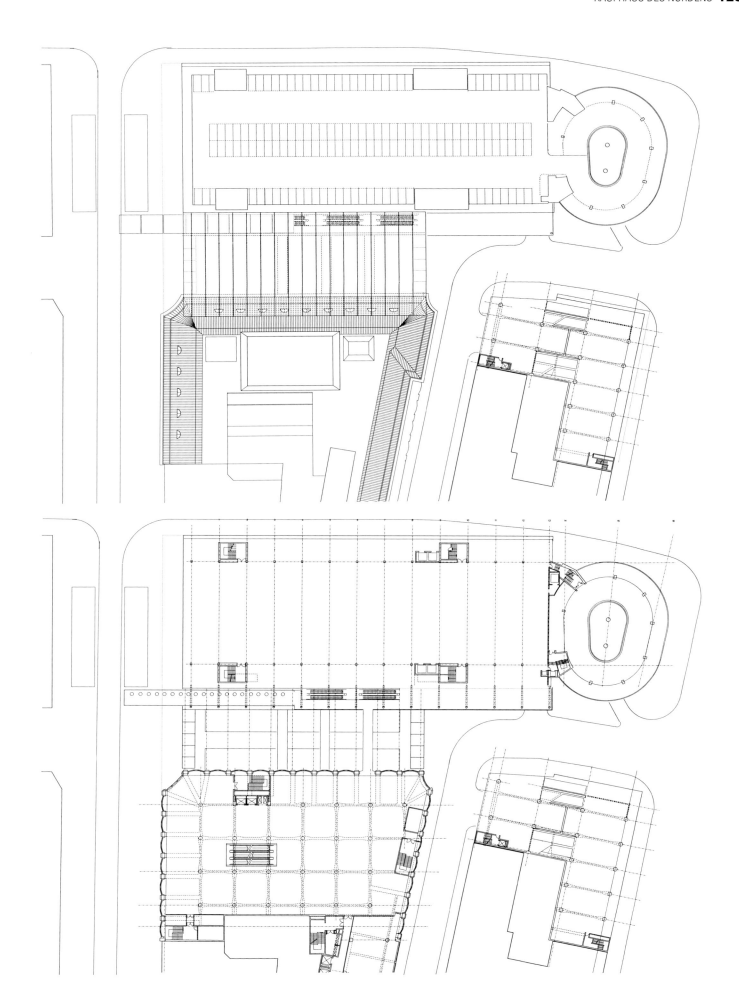

Opposite: Level one floor plan; Ground floor plan

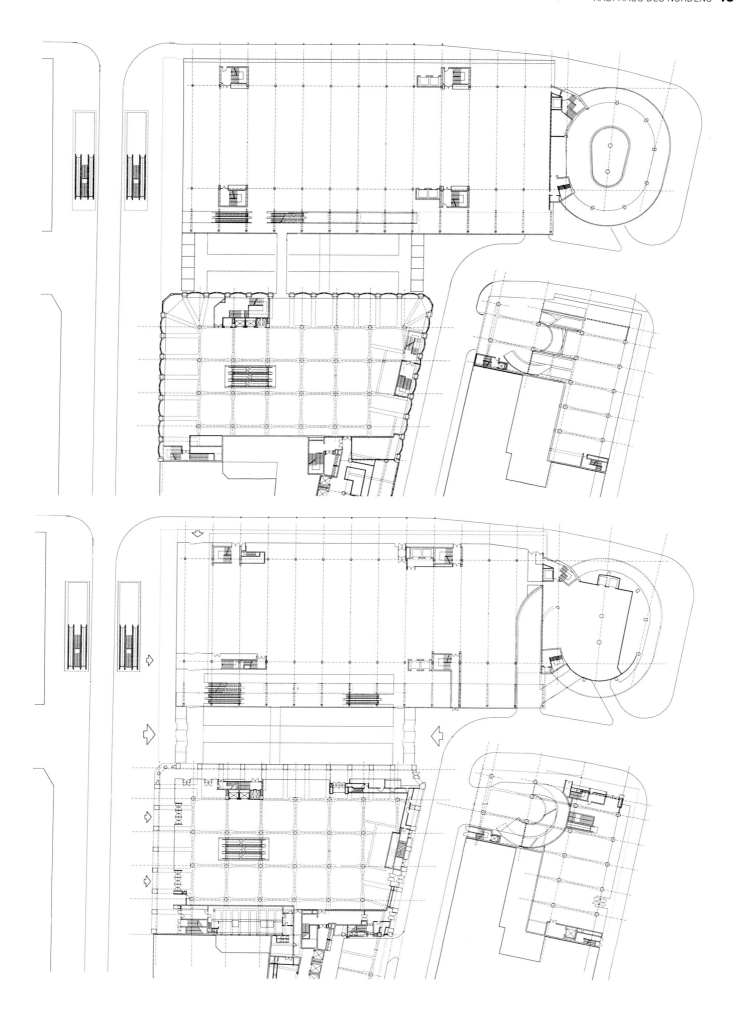

Opposite: First basement floor plan; Plan of existing parking area: 1. Roof (125 spaces), 2. Ramp (156), 3. Parkhouse Kaufhof (320).

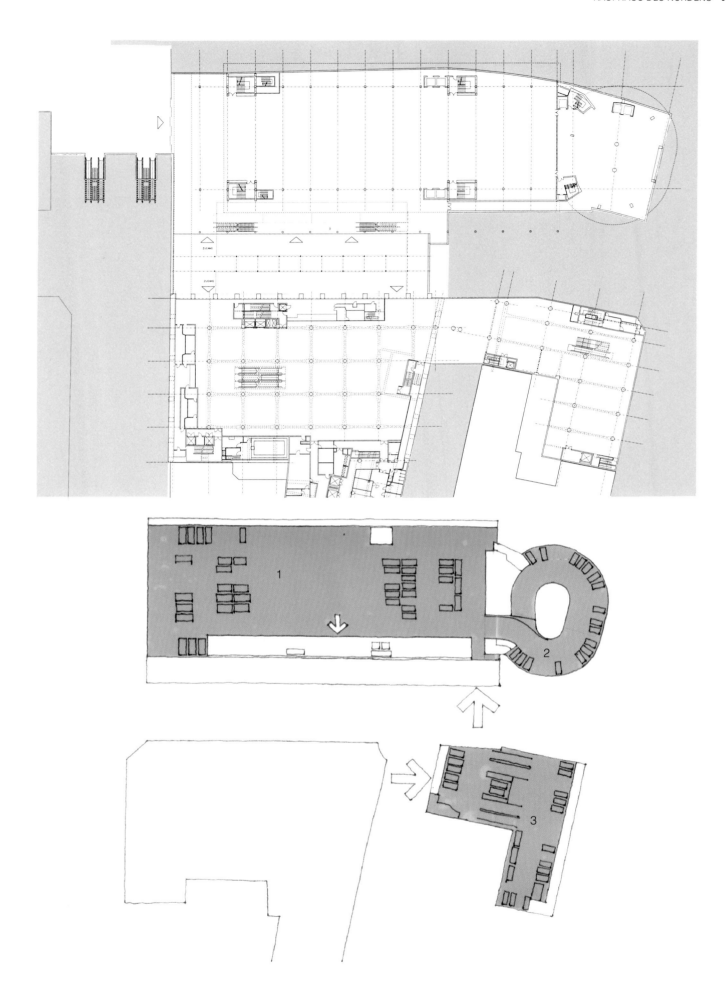

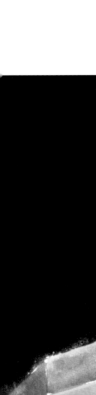

Opposite: New parking area proposal; New development of parkhouse: 1.Two new levels – 172 and 290 parking spaces, 2. Ramp – 156 and 54 additional spaces, 3. Parkhouse site available for different use. Total = 672; 4. Extended facade, 5. Possible access, 6. Area available for new development

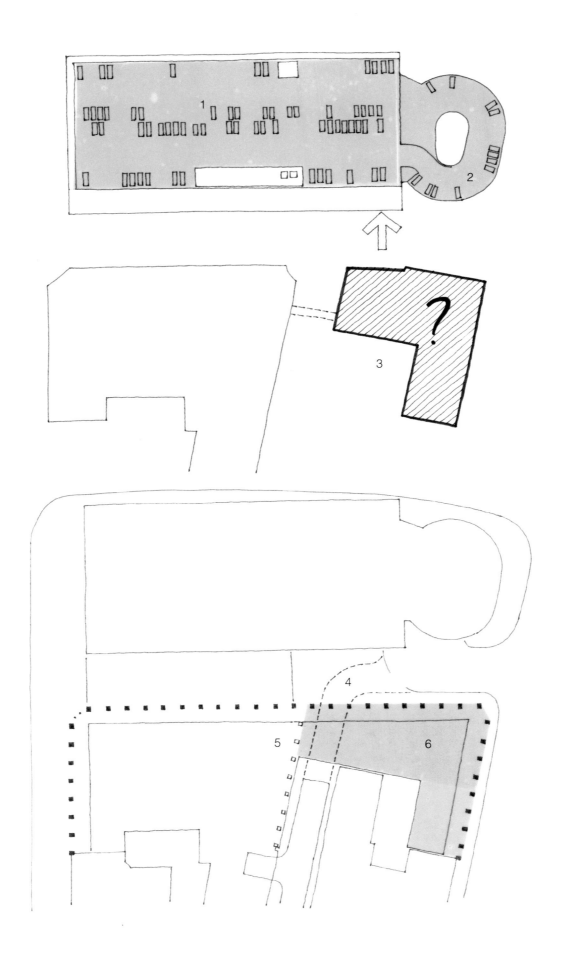

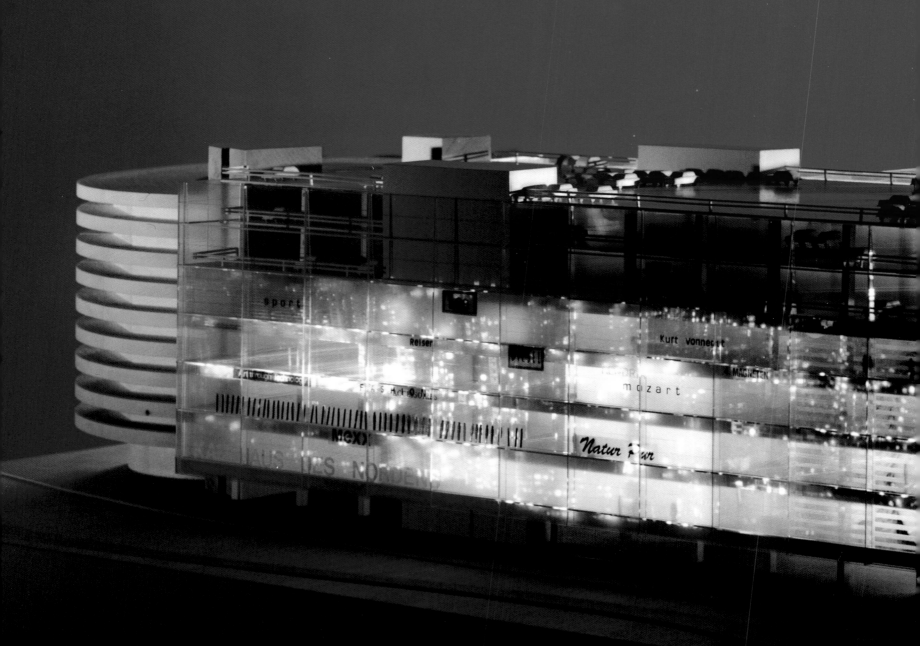

Opposite: Proposal for internal organisation: 1. Small scale lettable shop unit, 2. Large shop unit, 3. Concourse

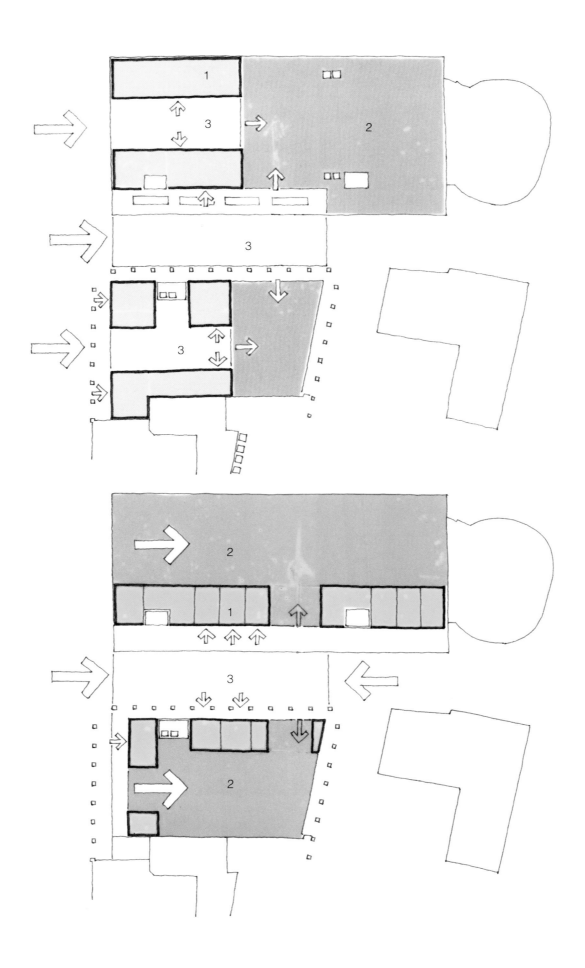

Opposite: South-west elevation; North-west elevation; Cross section; Longitudinal section

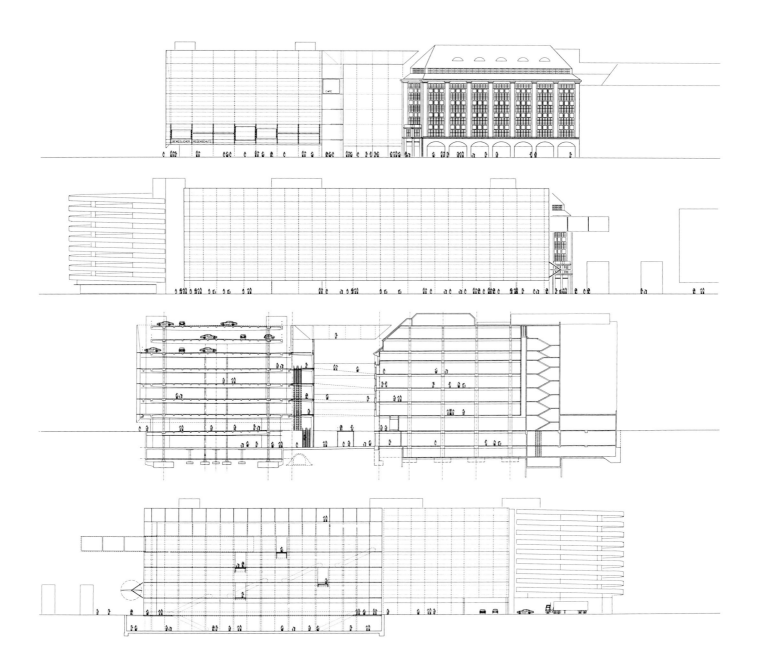

Opposite: 1. Natural ventilation, 2. Wind and rain protection, 3. Buffer zone, 4. Noise from road and railway, 5. Services – air (existing),
6. Natural light in basement, 7. Extended sprinkler, 8. Natural ventilation in atrium

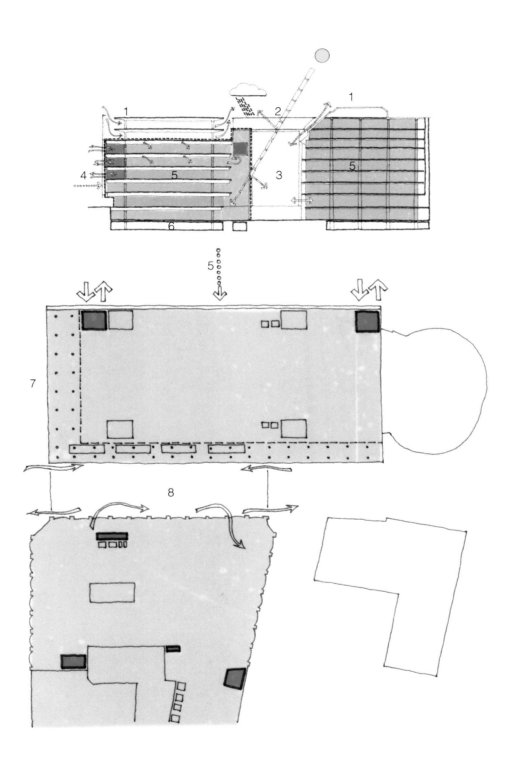

Biographies

WILLIAM ALSOP AADip SADG RIBA FRSA

Born: Northampton, England 1947

Qualifications:
Architectural Association Diploma
Member of the Royal Institute of British Architects
Société d'Architectes Diplômes par le Gouvernement
Fellow of the Royal Society of Arts
Bernard Webb Scholar, Rome
William van Allen Medal for Architecture, New York
Professor, Bremen Academy for Art and Music
Unit Master, Architectural Association

1973-77	Cedric Price Architects
1973-81	Tutor in Sculpture, St Martin's School of Art
1978-79	Roderick Ham Architects
1980-89	William Alsop Architects
1990-	Alsop & Störmer Architects. Offices in London, Hamburg, Moscow and East Anglia

JAN STÖRMER

Born: Berlin, Germany 1942

Qualifications:
Dipl Ing Architekt

1960-62	Engineering studies, Bremen
1964-69	Attended the Academy of Art, Hamburg
1969-70	Travelling and working in the USA
1969	Founder member of Me-di-um Architects, Hamburg
-89	Partner of Me-di-um Architects
1990-	Alsop & Störmer Architects.

Selected Projects

1982	Westminster Pier, London
	Arts Centre Riverside Studios, Hammersmith, London
1987	Shipfish Office Bridge over the Elbe, Hamburg
	Media Park, Cologne – Special prize
	Rainbow Quays Apartment, London Docklands
1988	Workshop and Apartment Complex, Hamburg
	New Art Museum, Hamburg
	Floating Pier with Library & Restaurant Citicorp, London

	BBC Arena Offices, London
	Lambeth Floating Fire Station, London
	Leisure Pool, Sheringham
	Hamburg Ferry Terminal
	Canary Wharf Eastern Access Control Building and Lifting Bridges, London
1989	Cardiff Bay Barrage, UK
1990	Hérouville St Clair Shopping Centre, La Tour Européene
	Cardiff Bay Visitors' Centre
	Port de la Lune, Garron Activator, Bordeaux
	Hotel du Département, Marseilles
	Amiens Urban Interventions
1991	North Greenwich Jubilee Line Underground Station
	Leipziger Platz, Potsdamer Platz, Berlin
	Tottenham Hale Railway Station
	Mineral Water Production Plant, Sylt-Quelle
	National Museum Extension, Nuremberg
	British Pavilion, Seville Exposition 1992
	Ship Museum, Bremen
	Nantes Boxes
	Urban Study, Nantes
1992	CrossRail Station, Paddington, London
	Boxing Hall, Berlin
	ASW–MSP Office Building, Sheffield
	Telecommunications Tower, Singapore
	Umweltbehörde, Hamburg

Awards / Competitions

1971	Centre Pompidou, Paris – 2nd prize
1982	Westminster Pier – 1st prize
1986	Shipfish Office Bridge over the Elbe, Hamburg
1987	Media Park, Cologne – Special prize
1988	Logistic Centre, Hamburg – 1st prize
1990	Hotel du Département, Marseilles – 1st prize
	UK Pavilion, Seville Exposition 1992 – 2nd prize
1991	Cardiff Bay Visitors' Centre, UK – RIBA Regional Award for Architecture, *Sunday Times* Royal Fine Art Commission
	Potsdamer/Leipziger Platz – 4th prize
1992	Cardiff Bay Visitors' Centre – RIBA National Award for Architecture
	'Berlin 2000' Boxing Hall – Commended 1st, disabled facilities